POLICE PATROL ALLOCATION AND DEPLOYMENT

Eric J. Fritsch

University of North Texas

John Liederbach

Bowling Green State University

Robert W. Taylor

University of North Texas

PEARSON

Prentice Hall

Upper Saddle River, New Jersey
Columbus, Ohio

Library of Congress Cataloging-in-Publication Data

Fritsch, Eric J.
  Police patrol allocation and deployment / Eric J. Fritsch, John Liederbach,
Robert W. Taylor.
      p. cm.
  Includes index.
  ISBN 0-13-513183-9
  1. Police patrol. 2. Police administration. I. Liederbach, John. II. Taylor, Robert W.
III. Title.
  HV8080.P2.F75 2008
  363.2'32—dc22

                                                                2007047114

Editor in Chief: Vernon R. Anthony
Senior Editor: Tim Peyton
Editorial Assistant: Alicia Kelly
Director of Marketing: David Gessell
Marketing Manager: Adam Kloza
Marketing Coordinator: Alicia Dysert
Production Manager: Kathy Sleys
Creative Director: Jayne Conte
Cover Design: Bruce Kenselaar
Cover Illustration/Photo: John Foxx/Super Stock
Full-Service Project Management/Composition: Yasmeen Neelofar/
    GGS Book Services
Printer/Binder: Courier Companies

Pearson Education LTD.
Pearson Education Australia PTY,
    Limited
Pearson Education Singapore, Pte. Ltd
Pearson Education North Asia Ltd

Pearson Education, Canada, Ltd
Pearson Educación de Mexico, S.A.
    de C.V.
Pearson Education–Japan
Pearson Education Malaysia, Pte. Ltd

PEARSON
Prentice
Hall

                                      10 9 8 7 6 5 4 3 2 1
                              ISBN-13: 978-0-13-513183-1
                              ISBN-10:   0-13-513183-9

POLICE PATROL ALLOCATION AND DEPLOYMENT

To my wife, Cheryl,
to my sons Jerod, Jacob, Jadyn, and Jaxon,
and my daughter Joley.
Eric J. Fritsch

To Allyson and Benjamin
John Liederbach

To my wife, Mary
Robert W. Taylor

CONTENTS

PREFACE

The patrol function is the cornerstone of modern policing. Surprisingly, however, current books in the policing area do not adequately cover patrol allocation and deployment issues. Texts have been written concerning a range of topics that are of interest to students, academicians, police administrators and training coordinators, including interview and interrogation, traffic enforcement, pursuit driving, crisis intervention, and use of force, to name a few. No text covers patrol allocation and deployment as central issues in the day-to-day management of police agencies and personnel. These issues are particularly important today, because most police agencies currently employ patrol allocation and deployment strategies that are woefully inadequate and/or outdated. So too, citizen demands regarding what the police should be doing and how they should "protect and serve" the public invariably evolve over time and are often dependent on shifting political and social realities, all of which influence the administrative decisions of police chiefs and other department executives concerning how patrol officers will accomplish their jobs.

Police administrators are in dire need of an information resource they can use in order to comprehensively consider the critical issues involved in patrol allocation and deployment, as well as inform them concerning the latest technologies designed to maximize the efficiency of patrol allocation and deployment strategies. Allocation and deployment issues are not simple or "cut and dried," but rather, inherently complex because police administrators must take into account a myriad of factors and concerns—both organizational and community-based—in order to both maximize departmental resources and adequately address the concerns and priorities of citizens that may disagree as to what problems police should address and how they should address them.

While this book will be of interest to police administrators and training coordinators, it will also be of interest to researchers who study issues of police effectiveness, especially the historical development of patrol as a major police function and the impact of patrol innovations on the function of the police. Finally, the book can be used as an ancillary text in classes specifically devoted to law enforcement issues, as well as police administration, including graduate courses concerning police behavior, effectiveness, and the role of law enforcement within the changing context of the twenty-first century.

This book presents a balanced overview concerning the primary patrol allocation and deployment issues, and is intended to provide a practical guide to making informed decisions using the latest available tools, research, and technology. It is also comprehensively researched and accessible to audiences of diverse professional, scholarly, and student backgrounds. This book also includes a discussion of the unique challenges associated with the deployment of special and nontraditional patrol units as well as future developments that are likely to alter the landscape of patrol deployment and allocation decision-making in the future.

ABOUT THE AUTHORS

Eric J. Fritsch is associate professor in the Department of Criminal Justice at the University of North Texas in Denton, TX. He has authored and coauthored several journal articles, books, book chapters, and technical reports. His articles have appeared in numerous journals including *Crime and Delinquency, Law and Policy, Criminal Justice Policy Review, Police Quarterly,* and the *American Journal of Criminal Law.* His areas of interest include juvenile justice and delinquency, gangs, criminological theory, law enforcement, criminal procedure, organizational assessment, and research methods. He is a former police officer and has worked extensively with law enforcement agencies for the past 15 years having conducted numerous studies on managerial and organizational practices, including allocation and deployment studies.

John Liederbach is associate professor in the Criminal Justice Program at Bowling Green State University. He received his Ph.D. in criminal justice from the University of Cincinnati, and he previously worked as an assistant professor in the Department of Criminal Justice at the University of North Texas. His primary research interest is police behavior, specifically variations in the street-level behavior of patrol officers across community types. Dr. Liederbach has also published articles related to the offending behavior of medical doctors and white-collar crime more generally. His work has appeared in various journals, including *Justice Quarterly, Policing: An International Journal of Police Strategies and Management, Criminal Justice Review, the American Journal of Criminal Justice,* and *Youth Violence and Juvenile Justice: An Interdisciplinary Journal.*

Robert W. Taylor is professor and chair of the Department of Criminal Justice at the University of North Texas in Denton, Texas. He has an extensive background in academic and professional criminal justice, having taught at four major universities and served as a sworn police officer and major crimes detective (in Portland, OR) for over 6 years. He has also authored and coauthored over one hundred articles, books, and manuscripts focusing on police administration, international and domestic terrorism, drug trafficking, internet crimes, and criminal justice policy. Robert W. Taylor has been the recipient of over $2 million in external grants and is an active consultant to various U.S. and international criminal justice agencies. He is an active member of the Academy of Criminal Justice Sciences and the American Society of Criminology.

Patrol Allocation and Deployment in Context

CHAPTER

1

Patrol Work: The Context of Allocation and Deployment Strategies

Law enforcement officers and citizens alike recognize patrol as the most prominent and important function of modern policing. Police officers invariably begin their careers as patrol officers, and the experience of being a "beat cop" forms a common thread that works to shape the shared perceptions and attitudes of all officers within the organization—from rookie cops to veteran homicide detectives up through department administrators. More than likely, they all had been patrol officers at one time or another and those who have been promoted to higher positions within the organization remain indelibly stamped by the experience. For their part, citizens continue to identify with the officer on the beat more than any other aspects of the police agency, probably because the patrol officer remains the most accessible way to invoke the law in times of crisis or obtain assistance when it is needed the most.

On average, municipal police agencies assign over 60 percent of all officers to patrol duty.[1] Routine patrol tends to dominate officer shift time regardless of variations across different types of police organizations and/or community contexts; that is, cops spend most of their time on routine patrol whether they work in crime-ridden urban neighborhoods, well-to-do suburban districts, or sparsely populated rural areas and small towns.[2] These truths provide evidence to the fact that patrol is a cornerstone of modern policing—something that is essential and basic to the law enforcement enterprise.

Surprisingly, however, current books in the policing area do not adequately cover patrol allocation and deployment issues. Competent texts have been written concerning a range of topics that are specifically aimed at police administrators and training coordinators, including interview and interrogation, traffic enforcement, pursuit driving, crisis intervention, and the use of force. However, no text covers patrol allocation and deployment as the central issues in the day-to-day management of police agencies and personnel. These issues are particularly important now, because most police agencies currently employ patrol allocation and deployment strategies that are inadequate or outdated. So too, citizen demands regarding what the police should be doing and how they should "protect and serve" the public invariably evolve over time and are often dependent on shifting political and social realities, all of which influence the administrative decisions of police chiefs and other department executives concerning how patrol officers will accomplish their jobs. Clearly, police executives are in need of an information resource that they can use in order to comprehensively consider the critical issues involved in patrol allocation and deployment, as well as to inform them about the latest technologies designed to maximize the efficiency of these strategies.

Allocation and deployment issues are not simple or "cut and dried," but rather, inherently complex because police administrators must take into account a myriad of factors and concerns—both organizational and community-based—in order to maximize departmental resources and adequately address the concerns and priorities of citizens that may disagree as to what problems police should address and how they should address them. Police administrators have only a finite amount of resources to do an infinite job. Given the nature of the police role, there is, for all practical purposes, no limit upon what a community might call upon police to do. Many agencies, for example, operating with a community policing philosophy, have become immersed in innumerable quality of life issues—from rehabilitating playgrounds to demolishing abandoned structures. The first issue a police administrator must face when making decisions about neighborhood responsiveness is "How much can I afford?" Quite obviously, every police agency has core responsibilities that must be met. These core responsibilities consume the vast majority of the resources available. After the core responsibilities are met, there are a number of options or other responsibilities that exist competing for the scarce proactive resources that are available. An agency might deploy community resource officers. There might be an organized, structured effort at problem-oriented endeavors. Officers might be assigned to schools, either as school resources officers or as Drug Abuse Resistance Education officers. Regular patrol officers might spend a portion of their time on foot patrol or bicycle patrol or even mounted patrol. Yet, another alternative is staffing storefronts. Beyond these possibilities for neighborhood responsiveness programs, there is concurrent demand to staff specialized units focused upon particular offenses or problem behaviors (e.g., gang units, traffic units, and crime response teams). The possibilities are, indeed, diverse, and difficult choices have to be made by police administrators.

This book presents a balanced overview concerning the primary patrol allocation and deployment issues, and is intended to provide a practical guide to making informed decisions using the latest available tools, research, and technology. Though the book covers some topics that are theoretical in nature, the text should primarily be viewed as a piece of applied research, or a means to present specific research information in order to aid police organizations in solving the practical problems related to patrol allocation and deployment.

PATROL ALLOCATION AND DEPLOYMENT DEFINED

This book specifically discusses two separate but interrelated concepts. The term *patrol allocation* refers to the issue of how many officers should be assigned to the patrol function in order to provide the level of service needed in any given jurisdiction or community. Decisions regarding allocation may be influenced by objectively based factors such as the number of citizen calls for service that are received by the department or the geographical area of the jurisdiction, among others. Allocation decisions are also driven by more subjective, policy-based factors. These can include the department's goals concerning officer response time to calls for service or whether or not the department employs one or two officer units in especially high-crime beats. While allocation decisions concern the issue of how many officers should be assigned, the term *patrol deployment* addresses the issue of where, when, and how these officers should be assigned. For example, what should officers do when they are not responding to calls for service? How should the department devise shift schedules in order to maximize manpower? What are the primary responsibilities of officers on patrol?

In order to create a meaningful context for the discussion of these issues, this introductory chapter aims to provide the reader with a thorough understanding concerning *why* the work of patrol officers, and by extension allocation and deployment decisions, is so crucial to the successful operation of any police department. The section below discusses the importance of patrol along several different dimensions, including: (1) the use of patrol as a means to accomplish many of the primary goals of police organizations, (2) patrol as an avenue or "gateway" to the rest of the criminal justice system, and (3) patrol as the primary way for police organizations to identify and address a wide variety of citizen concerns and public priorities. Following this discussion regarding the integral nature of patrol, an overview of the rest of the text, including brief outlines of the different sections and chapters of the book, is provided.

Why Patrol Matters

Patrol continues to be a core function of police because it has traditionally been viewed as a task associated with accomplishing the primary goals of most police organizations and officers. Some of the evidence concerning the importance of patrol can be gleaned from studies designed to document and record the workload of patrol officers, including when and how they interact with citizens. These studies not only inform us as to what we mean when we use the term "patrol work," but they also illustrate how thoroughly integrated patrol work is with what we more generally consider "police work," or the things that the public expects and demands from all law enforcement agencies.

The studies designed to document and record the workload of patrol officers have evolved over time and have utilized a number of methodologies including calls for service records, officer activity reports, and the direct observation of officers.[3] A major theme of the earliest studies concerning patrol officer workload involved dispelling the popular myth that police spend almost all of their time protecting the "thin blue line" between law and order.[4] These studies worked to dispel the notion that *all* the police do is fight crime, and they made researchers and the general public increasing cognizant of certain realities of patrol work that police themselves had long recognized. That is, while "crime fighting" remains law enforcement's primary mandate, a large percentage of the patrol officer's time is spent on tasks intended to address a wide variety of citizen demands that are only peripherally related to law enforcement.

Reviews of calls for service records revealed that only about half of all citizen requests involved crime-related matters, and a very small percentage of dispatched assignments involved crimes against persons. Instead, patrol officers performed a wide array of tasks, particularly service-related activities, and other tasks that are not commonly associated with crime fighting. Some examples of service-related tasks include providing medical assistance, addressing utility problems, controlling animals, and servicing disabled vehicles. Additional tasks include crowd control, policing domestic and nondomestic disputes, and juvenile problems.

Aside from identifying the almost endless array of problems handled by patrol officers, these studies also documented several "core" activities that consume most of the time patrol officers spend while they are not directly encountering citizens. For example, routine motorized patrol (or uncommitted patrol time) has been found to be the primary activity of officers across jurisdictions. In general, routine motor patrol consumes anywhere from 20 to 40 percent of total shift time.[5]

Why do police spend so much time "simply driving around" and waiting for a call for service? Routine patrol continues to consume a large percentage of patrol officers' time because it serves to address several of the primary goals of police work. For example, patrol creates a visible police presence in the community.[6] Police who are out on patrol are readily recognized by citizens because of distinctive uniforms and patrol cars. As such, patrol can work to promote an impression of safety among citizens, as well as reduce citizen fears concerning local neighborhood crime. The visible presence produced by patrol is also assumed to deter potential criminal offenders who should become more hesitant to offend within proximity of police. Patrol also works to decentralize, or "scatter," police across a given geographical area. Decentralization allows police to respond to citizen calls for service as quickly as possible because a patrol officer should be relatively close to the location of any caller. Routine patrol allows officers to be available or "in-service" and ready to respond to emergencies whose exact nature, location, and time of occurrence remain unknown to both the police administrator and the officer on the beat.

Finally, these workload studies identified other, less glamorous "core" activities that police administrators must nonetheless account for in any allocation and deployment strategy. These primarily include time spent on report writing and other administrative tasks, on driving en route to and from specific locations, and on personal breaks and meals. Administrative tasks such as report writing generally consume about one-quarter of all the time patrol officers spend alone on shift, although officers employed by large organizations appear to spend considerably more time on administrative tasks than those from smaller departments. Meals and personal breaks can be expected to take up anywhere from 10 to 30 percent of the shift time officers spend while not encountering citizens.[7]

Patrol Officers as Gatekeepers

Aside from serving to accomplish many of the tasks commonly associated with police agencies, patrol officers also perform an integral role as "gate-keepers" to the criminal justice system. Patrol officers are usually the first point of contact between citizens and the system, and their decisions concerning how and when to intervene frequently dictate whether or not, and if so how, the system will process individual citizens. Patrol officers exercise wide-scale discretion and the ability to make decisions in the absence of direct supervision. Patrol officer discretion appears to be most heavily influenced by legal factors such as seriousness of the offense, the presence or absence of evidence of wrongdoing, or the preferences of the complainant.[8] However, there is also considerable evidence to suggest that extralegal factors such as citizen demeanor, social class, gender, and race also influence officer decision-making on occasion.[9]

Unlike most corporations or other types of business organizations, some of the most important decisions to be made by law enforcement organizations—such as which laws to enforce, when an arrest should be made, and when a suspect should be handled informally rather than arrested—are most often made at the street level by patrol officers rather than by those in the higher ranks of the police organization. As Davis points out in his discussion regarding the importance of patrol officer discretion within the wider organizational context, enforcement policy is made primarily by the officer on the beat during his or her daily interactions with citizens.[10]

The Patrol Mandate: Organizational Goals and Meeting Citizen Demands

The overview above illustrates the importance of patrol along several dimensions. First, we know that patrol is important because it consumes the bulk of officer personnel resources. Moreover, the visible police presence produced by patrol makes citizens feel safer. More generally, the patrol function serves as the primary means to accomplish goals that are common to all police departments and officers, including deterrence and rapid response to citizen calls for service. Finally, by virtue of their street-level presence, patrol officers act as "gatekeepers" to the wider criminal justice system, often times using their discretion in order to determine what laws get enforced and which suspects will formally enter the system through an arrest.

Perhaps of more direct concern to police administrators and others who are in-charge of directing patrol units is the fact that patrol and the work of patrol officers remains the primary means by which police organizations can identify and address a wide variety of citizen concerns and public priorities. The organization must devise strategies and tactics to utilize the limited manpower and resources of the department and satisfy citizen concerns that are almost limitless. For example, what percentage of time should patrol officers spend on traffic enforcement? Should patrol officers be expected to rapidly respond every time a commercial or residential burglary alarm goes off? Should patrol officers use some of their "uncommitted" time on crime prevention activities such as school patrols or attending community meetings? The authors' previous involvement in a project designed to assess the effectiveness of one large metropolitan police department can be used as a guide as to how we can begin to address these issues.

A few years ago, the authors were asked to conduct an operations analysis of a large police agency, hereafter to be referred to as the Southwest Police Department (SWPD). The department's command staff had requested increased funding for more officers from the city council, and the council engaged the authors as consultants to provide an outside review of the department's operations. The SWPD patrols a jurisdiction with over half a million residents and is located within one of the nation's largest metropolitan regions. The department can be characterized as a progressive agency that has embraced the community-oriented policing (COP) concept and many of its corollary strategies and tactics.

For example, each of the city's patrol beats is staffed by an officer that has been designated as a community policing "specialist." The department maintains a Citizen Police Academy and a Citizens on Patrol program. The SWPD also operates specific programs for schools, including drug abuse education courses and school security programs. The department's organizational structure includes multiple storefront "mini-stations" that are designed to further enhance connections between the local neighborhoods and the SWPD. More so than many other departments, the SWPD clearly recognizes the importance of fostering strong connections with the local community. The SWPD has backed this philosophy with the implementation of real programs designed to satisfy the goals common to all community policing initiatives—tactics and strategies designed to engage citizens and communities as "co-producers" in crime control and community order.[11]

Yet, despite the modern, progressive character of the SWPD, the department was challenged by city council to "prove" that it needed more officers. Despite the existence of well-publicized and supported community programs, citizens and the city government wanted to ensure that the SWPD could also deliver other, more traditional services. Specifically, the authors were charged with producing advice concerning how the department could do the following: (1) increase the visibility of patrol officers, (2) provide enough patrol officers in order to immediately respond to emergencies, and (3) provide enough patrol officers to adequately respond to non-emergencies. In an era where police administrators are challenged to devise and implement new strategies and tactics that are intended to increase community collaboration and crime prevention goals, the city council and citizens of Southwest city were reminding the department of their original law enforcement mandate; community policing is a fine goal, but those new programs were viewed as important priorities *in addition to* the traditional goals of patrol responsiveness and visibility.

As part of the authors' review of the department, they met with community representatives, government officials, and SWPD officers and administrators. They also conducted surveys of Southwest city residents and department personnel concerning a range of issues relevant to documenting and improving the operations of the SWPD. The results of the citizen surveys speak volumes concerning not only the importance of meeting a wide variety of citizen concerns through patrol but also as to why so many police administrators feel as though patrol levels are continually at the "breaking point"—a situation where the department's limited patrol resources can no longer meet increasing demands on patrol officer time.

For example, survey respondents were asked their opinion regarding how important fifteen different types of problems were in the city and for the police department. Over 90 percent of the 400 survey respondents believed that six of the fifteen types of problems were "important" or "very important," including property crime (94.5 percent), violent crime (93.8 percent), youth gangs (91.3 percent), traffic offenses (91 percent), unsupervised juveniles (90.3 percent), and drug use (90.1 percent). In addition, over three-fourths of the respondents believed that seven of the remaining nine types of problems were "important" or "very important," including school related problems (87.5 percent), the appearance of neighborhoods (84.8 percent), public intoxication (83.8 percent), prostitution (80.6 percent), homeless persons (79.1 percent), abandoned buildings (78.3 percent), and problems with neighbors (74.6 percent). These results are consistent with citizen surveys that have been conducted in other jurisdictions.[12] Citizens invariably view traditional crime control problems as law enforcement's primary priority, however, they also appear to be very reluctant to rate any sort of problem or activity as a "low priority" for the police. In short, citizens feel that it is important for police to address *every* sort of problem whether it is related specifically to crime fighting or not.

If it is accurate to say that citizens view almost all types of problems as important for the police to address, what kind of strategies does the public want the police to enact in order to reduce these problems? Again, data from our study is instructive. Citizens were asked to rate how important different strategies were to improving the performance of the SWPD. Citizens believed that it was either "important" or "very important" for the SWPD to utilize traditional strategies such as hiring more patrol officers (84.8 percent) and responding more quickly to calls for service (95.5 percent), but they also believed that it was "important" or "very important" for the SWPD to concurrently provide additional training (93.6 percent), incorporate new technology (90.6 percent), and enact tactics designed to improve both community relations in general (94.5 percent) and specific police relations with minority groups in the community (90.8 percent).

Through the survey and other assessment tools used in their study, citizens were able to provide them with a clear understanding about what the public demands from the police through the patrol function; citizens believe that almost every type of problem is important for the police to address, and they believe that the police should use a wide variety of tactics and strategies to address the problems whether they directly involve fighting crime, addressing community disorder, or engaging in collaborative strategies with citizens. From a research perspective, the results of the citizen survey were encouraging. Citizens did not appear to be alienated from the SWPD, but rather, they believed the department was capable of addressing their concerns. From the perspective of a police administrator, however, the citizen survey results could be interpreted as daunting—how are the police supposed to address every sort of problem and meet the seemingly never-ending demands of citizens? How can the police stretch their limited resources to apply a wide range of tactics and strategies to confront these community issues? How can the police concurrently accomplish specific organizational objectives that are integral to the functioning of the department but may be of little concern to citizens?

Patrol allocation and deployment strategies provide an avenue to begin to address these exact issues. Patrol allocation and deployment should be viewed as a means to an end—an avenue for police administrators to address these concerns in the most efficient way possible. Administrators increasingly face an organizational landscape that is constantly changing, not only in terms of objectively based factors such as how many calls for service the department must answer or what type of crime problems are emerging within their own jurisdiction, but also large-scale changes in patrol philosophies that are likely to significantly impact the day-to-day operation of the organization, such as the emergence of the COP model a few decades ago. Absent specific knowledge concerning modern allocation and deployment strategies, it is unlikely that police agencies will be able to meet the patrol mandate and satisfy both organizational and citizen demands.

Organization of the Book

While this chapter demonstrates the central importance of patrol allocation and deployment to a wide range of audiences, chapter 2 provides a comprehensive review of the existing research on patrol effectiveness and issues concerning how to optimally allocate police resources. The review takes the reader through the literature that concerns issues of central importance to the policing profession, including the issue of how much the police can affect crime, whether or not patrol can accomplish the sometimes disparate goals associated with various police functions, and what are the most viable means to maximize the efficiency and effectiveness of patrol.

Chapter 3 traces the history of various patrol allocation and deployment models from those used at the beginning of the modern professional era of policing to those used more recently, including allocation by geography, allocation by hazard formula, allocation by queuing models, allocation for the prevention of crime, the Patrol Car Allocation Model (PCAM), the Patrol Allocation Model (PAM), and the Allocation Model for Police Patrol (AMPP). The chapter concludes by summarizing the strengths and weaknesses of allocation models. Chapter 4 begins with an overview of the most recent patrol allocation model, specifically the Model for the Allocation of Patrol Personnel (MAPP), a comprehensive, web-based patrol allocation model created by the authors. The chapter then focuses on providing the reader a "roadmap" for understanding patrol allocation decisions by identifying the factors that are likely to influence the number of patrol officers who are needed to accomplish various organizational objectives. These factors include variables that are primarily "data-driven" (e.g., number of calls for service, average service time, jurisdictional size, etc.) and those that are "policy-driven" (e.g., performance objectives, patrol priorities, and administrative time). The chapter concludes by providing the reader a detailed example to demonstrate how the MAPP can be used to inform police administrative decisions concerning patrol allocation.

The remaining chapters primarily focus on patrol deployment issues, including scheduling, modern tactical deployment approaches, and evolving operational deployment strategies. Chapter 5 begins with an overview concerning the importance of implementing an effective scheduling plan to police administrators and the goal of maximizing deployment benefits. The chapter outlines the strengths and weaknesses of various scheduling plans, including 5-8 scheduling, 4-10 scheduling, 3-12 scheduling, and other alternative scheduling plans. The chapter concludes with a discussion of other key scheduling issues, including shift rotation, days off rotation, and proportional scheduling. Chapter 6 covers modern tactical deployment approaches, including directed patrol, hot spots patrol, and aggressive patrol and zero-tolerance tactics.

Over the course of the last thirty years, policing has experienced a remarkable period of reform. Chapter 7 details how this reform movement has led to the development of several operational deployment strategies and models that have impacted police patrol allocation and deployment in general, especially the growing trend toward problem solving, community engagement, and the use of CompStat. As policing moves forward in the twenty-first century, can we expect similar changes and renewed calls for reform that may fundamentally alter patrol deployment and allocation decisions? The authors suggest how issues that have emerged since 9/11 and the advent of the "war on terror" may impact the future of patrol allocation and deployment.

ENDNOTES

1. M. J. Hickman and B. A. Reaves, *Local Police Departments, 2003* (Washington, D.C.: Bureau of Justice Statistics, 2006).

2. J. Frank, S. G. Brandl, and R. C. Watkins, "The Content of Community Policing: A Comparison of the Daily Activities of Community and Beat Officers," *Policing: An International Journal of Police Strategy and Management* 20, no. 4 (1997): 716–28; R. B. Parks, S. Mastrofski, C. Dejong, and M. K. Gray , "How Officers Spend Their Time with the Community," *Justice Quarterly* 16, no. 3 (1999): 483–518; J. Liederbach, "Addressing the 'Elephant in the Living Room': An Observational Study of the Work of Suburban Police," *Policing: An International Journal of Police Strategy and Management* 28, no. 3 (2005): 415–34.

3. G. W. Cordner, "Police Patrol Work Load Studies: A Review and Critique," *Police Studies* 2 (1979): 50–60; E. Cummings, I. Cummings, and L. Edell, "Policeman as a Philosopher, Friend, and Guide," *Social Problems* 12 (1965): 276–86; Frank et al., "The Content of Community Policing"; G. Kelling, T. Pate, D. Dieckman, and C. Brown, *The Kansas City Preventive Patrol Experiment: A Summary Report* (Washington, D.C.: Police Foundation, 1974); Liederbach, "Addressing the 'Elephant in the Living Room'"; Parks,

et al., "How Officers Spend Their Time with the Community"; A. J. Reiss, *The Police and the Public* (New Haven, CT: Yale University Press, 1974); G. P. Whitaker, "What Is Patrol Work," *Police Studies* 4, no. 4 (1982): 13–22.

4. T. Bercal , "Calls for Police Assistance: Consumer Demands for Government Service," *American Behavioral Scientist* 13 (1970): 680–90; Cummings et al., "Policeman as a Philosopher, Friend, and Guide"; Reiss, *The Police and the Public*; J. Q. Wilson, *Varieties of Police Behavior* (Cambridge, MA: Harvard University Press, 1968).

5. Frank et al., "The Content of Community Policing"; Liederbach, "Addressing the 'Elephant in the Living Room' "; Parks et al., "How Officers Spend Their Time with the Community."

6. R. H. Langworthy and L. F. Travis, *Policing in America: A Balance of Forces*, 3rd ed. (Upper Saddle River, NJ: Prentice Hall, 2003); S. Walker and C. M. Katz, *Police in America: An Introduction*, 5th ed. (New York: McGraw Hill, 2005).

7. Liederbach, "Addressing the 'Elephant in the Living Room' "; J. Liederbach and J. Frank, "Policing Mayberry: The Work Routines of Small-Town and Rural Officers," *American Journal of Criminal Justice* 28, no. 1 (2003): 53–72.

8. D. Black, "The Social Organization of Arrest," *Stanford Law Review* 23

(1971): 1087–1111; R. Lundman, R. Sykes, and J. Clark, "Police Control of Juveniles: A Replication," *Journal of Research in Crime and Delinquency* 15, no. 1 (1978): 74–91.

9. R. Lundman, "City Police and Drunk Driving: Baseline Data," *Justice Quarterly* 15 (1998): 527–46; D. A. Smith and C. A. Visher, "Street-Level Justice: Situational Determinants of Police Arrest Decisions," *Social Problems* 29, no. 2 (1981): 167–77; R. E. Sykes, J. C. Fox, and J. P. Clark, "A Socio-Legal Theory of Police Discretion," in *The Ambivalent Force: Perspectives on the Police*, ed. A. Niederhoffer and A. S. Blumberg, 2nd ed. (Hinsdale, Il: Dryden Press, 1974).

10. K. C. Davis, *Police Discretion* (St. Paul, MN: West Publishing, 1975).

11. D. H. Bayley, *Policing for the Future* (New York: Oxford University Press, 1994); J. E. Eck and W. Spellman, *Problem Solving: Problem-Oriented Policing in Newport News* (Washington, D.C.: National Institute of Justice, 1988); G. Kelling and M. H. Moore, "The Evolving Strategy of Policing," *Perspectives on Policing* (Washington, D. C.: National Institute of Justice, 1988).

12. K. Beck, N. Boni, and J. Packer, "The Use of Public Attitude Surveys: What Can They Tell Police Managers?" *Policing: An International Journal of Police Strategy and Management* 22, no. 2 (1999): 191–216.

CHAPTER

2

What We Know from Research on Police Patrol

How do the police affect crime? Is police patrol effective at catching criminals, responding to calls for service, and increasing citizen safety? What is the best way to maximize the efficiency and effectiveness of patrol through appropriate allocation and deployment measures? How many officers are necessary to adequately patrol a beat, neighborhood, or city? These questions are difficult to answer for police researchers and police administrators; nonetheless, officers are still deployed on a daily basis in cars, on motorcycles and bikes, and on foot, charged with the task of patrolling the neighborhoods and streets of the communities they serve. The majority of a police agency's budget is dedicated to patrol and patrol support functions. Since the formation of modern police forces, patrol is consistently recognized as the "backbone" of policing.[1] The majority of sworn personnel in an agency are assigned to the patrol function which delivers the bulk of police services to the public.[2]

This chapter consists of four main sections. In the first section, the current state of knowledge based on police research is assessed and challenges to some of the research findings are offered. In the second section, the fundamental objectives of patrol are identified, including visibility, rapid response, and immediate availability to respond to emergencies. In the third section, the literature on the impact of patrol on crime is discussed. In the final section of this chapter, a myriad of recent patrol deployment strategies designed to increase the efficiency and effectiveness of patrol operations are briefly discussed.

PATROL RESEARCH: CRITICISMS AND CONTRADICTIONS

There are numerous issues and methodological problems with the research conducted to date on police patrol and its effectiveness. For example, one criticism voiced by police officials is that police research tends to have a "big city" bias or an exclusive "East coast" focus.[3] Hence, patrol strategies and innovative programs that might very well be effective in the densely populated East coast of the United States might be ineffective in other locales. Foot patrol, for example, has found success in densely populated, northeastern cities. However, foot patrol is not an effective use of resources in many of the sprawling, less densely populated cities located west of the Mississippi such as Houston or Los Angeles, and it is certainly not a viable option in rural jurisdictions.

Perhaps the most salient issue with police research is the overgeneralization of the findings. For example, the Minneapolis Domestic Violence Experiment found that among various alternatives, arrest was the most effective method to reduce future domestic violence.[4] The study led to the adoption of mandatory arrest policies in many states, jurisdictions, and police departments. Unlike most policing studies, the research was replicated in a variety of cities across the country. The results of the original experiment were not confirmed in other cities, and in one city arrest *increased* future assaults.[5] Similarly, much of the research on police patrol is limited to a single location and has not been replicated. Finally, the bulk of police research over the past 20 years has been more concerned with what has not worked rather than what has worked. As a result, generalizations and summary conclusions regarding what works and what doesn't have typically not been supported by thorough empirical research.

Skolnick and Bayley aptly summarize the thinking regarding police research on patrol allocation and deployment in what is referred to as the "pre-CompStat era":

- First, increasing the number of police does not necessarily reduce crime rates or raise the proportion of crimes solved;
- Second, random motorized patrolling neither reduces crime nor improves chances of catching suspects;
- Third, two-person patrol cars are no more effective than one-person cars in reducing crime or catching criminals;
- Fourth, saturation patrolling does reduce crime, but only temporarily, largely by displacing it to other areas;
- Fifth, the kind of crime that terrifies Americans most—mugging, robbery, burglary, rape, and homicide—is rarely encountered by police on patrol;
- Sixth, improving response time to emergency calls has no effect on the likelihood of arresting criminals or even in satisfying involved citizens;
- Seventh, crimes are not solved—in the sense of offenders arrested and prosecuted—through criminal investigations conducted by police departments.[6]

These summary findings indicate that the main strategies used by police departments in the United States are not effective at reducing crime or reassuring the public.[7] Numerous researchers echo the observations of Skolnick and Bayley in one form or another.[8] In commenting on the state of police research, Strecher notes that, "In science, all knowledge is provisional. The essence of science is the verification and advancement of what is already known with repeated and refined research. The value of most police research findings is limited by a lack of both replication and refinement of the research."[9] What is perhaps most disturbing is that despite these and other conclusions, police agencies continue to engage in the tactics that the science concludes "don't work." Why do rational, high-level police executives still engage in tactics that the research says does not work? The answer is multifold.

First, the body of research upon which the above conclusions are drawn is anything but conclusive. As we noted earlier, many of the assumptions concerning the state of police research are based on one-time, decades-old studies that have not been replicated. In addition, only some of the goals of the police tactics studied were assessed. For example, rapid response was assessed based on its ability to apprehend criminals and increase public satisfaction with the police. While it might be true that a person would be as satisfied (if not more so) by a response that comes 45 minutes after a crime as long as they get a response, what about other types of calls? For instance, is a 45-minute response appropriate for a serious injury car accident? What about a call involving a child who can't breathe? Or an in-progress violent domestic call? How many lives have been saved by a rapidly responding police officer? How many injuries have been prevented? Assessing the value of rapid response only on the dynamic of apprehending criminals is myopic, and to conclude that it is not important at all for a police agency to rapidly respond to calls for service seems inappropriate at best. The research on rapid response did lead to numerous advances in call stacking, computer-aided dispatch, and other tactics designed to increase the efficiency of patrol operations and citizen satisfaction with police. However, there are still many circumstances that require a rapid response from the police, such as in-progress violent crimes. Therefore, the quest to respond rapidly to calls for service should not be abandoned altogether and should be a major factor in the allocation and deployment of patrol officers.

Second, we may be asking too much of the police in terms of reducing fear, especially given the observed disconnect between levels of fear and actual crime and the limited capacity of the police to respond to citizen fears directly. It is well known that those who fear crime the most have the least to fear. Since all crimes are not suppressible by police on patrol, should patrol be accountable for reducing citizen fear of crime? Significant fear reduction by police, who cannot possibly contact all of the citizens they police on a daily basis, is probably impossible given the current context of policing. More fundamentally, is fear reduction a legitimate goal of patrol?

Third, the comment that crimes are almost never solved by police is not entirely accurate. Crimes are solved by the police. Perhaps not the majority of crimes, but crimes are solved nonetheless. The notion that criminal investigation doesn't solve all crimes perhaps doesn't matter given that a major function of criminal investigation is to prepare cases for prosecution. Detectives continue to play a significant role in preparing witnesses, victims, paperwork, and evidence into a cohesive case ready for prosecution, so it seems inappropriate to focus solely on the issue of whether detectives are effective "crime solvers."

Fourth, although the research on one- vs. two-officer patrol units is well designed, replicated, and fairly clear, there are still violent, crime-ridden areas in certain cities where it is probably a good idea to have two-officer patrol units. In other words, although the efficiency of deploying one-officer units is well documented, there still might be logical reasons why certain units should be staffed with two officers. The research focused on whether two-officer units, in comparison to one-officer units, increased arrests and reduced crime, but what about officer "perceptions" of safety? Is it justifiable to neglect officer feelings of safety while working in certain areas of our communities? In sum, although the observations and assumptions cited by Skolnick and Bayley[10] might be quite true, the police are still patrolling, still investigating, still responding quickly to calls for service, and still affecting or reducing the crime rate.

The conclusion that "nothing works" in policing has not been satisfactorily addressed. The growing popularity of CompStat feeds the debate. The overwhelming reduction in crime in New York City following CompStat's introduction in 1994 cannot reasonably be attributed to anything but proactive policing that involves focused police interdictions through the development of appropriate deployment strategies. The growing CompStat philosophy concludes that the police are primarily responsible for the management and processing of crime, not the quality of life or fear of the residents they police. Indeed, it is obvious that adding more police officers or resources without adequate support, direction, and information will not reduce crime or improve police service. Research has revealed that directed, information-driven patrol tactics have led to significant reductions in crime.[11] Given these findings, existing criticisms of the overall effectiveness of patrol in reducing crimes seem to have been overstated.

PATROL: THE BIG PICTURE

Patrol remains the most visible and readily recognized function of modern police.[12] Depending on the level of specialization, approximately 60 percent of the sworn personnel in a police agency are assigned to patrol operations. Whether it is gauged in terms of the number of officers on patrol, the patrol budget, or the fact that patrol is the most visible component of law enforcement, patrol is the mainstay of police work.[13] Kelling neatly summarized the importance of patrol by stating, "From their initiation in England and America during the 19th century, police organizations have positioned police officers in communities for the purpose of patrolling predesignated areas conspicuously. The presence of readily identifiable police officers was presumed to prevent crime and disorder and to reassure citizens that, if crime and disorder did occur, police would be available to help them."[14]

O. W. Wilson argued that the basic purpose of patrol was the elimination of criminal opportunity. From his perspective, patrol is an indispensable service that plays a leading role in the accomplishment of the police purpose.[15] The basic philosophy behind Wilson's ideal of patrol was to create an impression of "omnipresence"; the perception that the police are present in all places at all times. Wilson was convinced that although a thief's desire to steal is not diminished, the opportunity to successfully carry out the theft is hampered by the presence of a police officer.[16] As discussed in Chapter 1, while deterrence is seen as a basic goal of patrol, the apprehension of offenders, the recovery of stolen property, and the provision of public service have also been identified as goals of patrol.[17] Meagher (1985) found that department size and location had little effect on the actual operation and core tasks of patrol that included law enforcement, order maintenance, service provision, and crime prevention.[18] In addition, as Sherman observes, the police have strayed little from the eighteenth-century philosophy of patrolling to detect crimes in progress and investigating those already completed.[19]

Recent technological advances in patrol have not necessarily translated to improved performance. In many respects, the introduction of new technologies in policing has been a double-edged sword; it has sometimes worked to forge greater ties among police and citizens, but also has led to increased expectations. While technology completed the link between police and citizens, it also increased the desire and need for police services. Typical patrol work is dominated by communication technology and, as a result, typical patrol is call-for-service dominated, reactive, and incident-based.[20] Despite community policing, patrol officers are still dominated by responding to calls for service and, when not on a call, are typically doing little in the way of *directed* crime prevention. When incidents occur, whether routine or emergency, they are usually the first to arrive, and thus must deal with people in the most agitated emotional conditions and confusing situations.[21] Most calls are citizen-initiated with officers initiating about 15 percent of all citizen contacts.[22] On average, the police make a self-initiated arrest only once in every fifteen tours of duty, or once in every 3 weeks.[23] Most time-based studies of police behavior have found that up to 50 percent of patrol time is uncommitted and is used for "patrolling."[24]

So what does the public expect patrol officers to do when not responding to calls for service? As discussed in chapter 1, the possibilities are endless but community responsiveness is the mandate. While there may be a variety of demands from the various neighborhoods or interest groups, be assured that in aggregate every American community will want three things from their police agency: (1) *immediate availability* to respond to emergencies, (2) *reasonable response times* even to nonemergencies, and (3) some level of *visibility* to provide feelings of security. These remain the essential elements of patrol allocation, deployment, and scheduling.

There is a constant strain between maintaining availability and quality handling of incidents. Incidents are frequently handled expediently, community policing philosophy or not. Officers are expected to "get back in service." Today, patrol officers must remain available for immediate dispatch to true emergencies just as in decades past. Indeed, maintaining immediate availability for genuine 911 emergencies is a primary mandate of each police agency. It is at the core of community responsiveness. And problem-oriented policing (POP) or community-oriented policing (COP) did not change that mandate. The best way to meet the mandate to maintain immediate availability is to deploy officers in patrol cars, spread them across a jurisdiction, and keep them in those cars. Hence, patrol is still patrol.

Rapid response is also fundamental to patrol operations because citizens demand it. Citizens who are stressed, distraught, upset, and in potential harm's way do not want to sit and wait for an hour for a patrol unit. They expect an officer to respond quickly. Critics of police chiefs who still show concern about response time would do well to listen to their own rhetoric. They are the same people who insist that police agencies "listen to their citizens, are responsive to citizen demands, maintain full and open communication," and the like. Ask any group of citizens what one of their primary expectations of a police agency is, and one can hear "rapid response in emergencies." Hence, patrol is still patrol.

Similarly, visibility is an essential concern of citizens. Clearly, citizens like to see police officers as they carry out their daily activities. They also like to see police officers in their neighborhoods. It is important for the police to be visible to citizens in order to make citizens feel safe and to deter potential criminal activity. As police administrators make patrol allocation and deployment decisions, embedded in these decisions are the enduring purposes of patrol-visibility, rapid response, and the need to maintain units always available on emergency stand-by. This same statement could have been written 30 years ago, but it is just as salient today. So 35 years after the Kansas City Preventive Patrol Experiment, 25 years after Herman Goldstein's "Crime and Delinquency" article describing POP, and 20 years after the emergence of community policing as recommended "standard operating procedure," patrol is still patrol. The type of calls patrol officers respond to have not changed. The relative frequency of call types is still the same; mostly it is dispute resolution, mostly among people who know each other. POP or no POP, patrol officers still return to the same addresses again and again. Most importantly, between handling calls for service, officers mostly do routine, nondirected patrol.

HOW DOES PATROL EFFECT CRIME?

Kelling, in discussing how to define the bottom line in policing, noted the following:

> A basic purpose of police is crime prevention. The idea that police cannot do anything about crime and that they stand helpless in the face of demographics, drugs, gangs, or whatever is unacceptable—often . . . a "cop-out" that covers lack of strategic commitment and absence of planning and implementation.[25]

A revisionist philosophy concludes that police agencies can impact the level of crime and disorder in a community. The police *do* make a difference. Saying that crime and disorder are products of social and economic forces the police cannot and should not affect is rejected.[26]

The causes of crime are by no means clear, and the police probably shouldn't concern themselves in such debates. "The ability of the police to 'solve' the crime problem is extremely limited. The 'crime problem' will not, indeed cannot, be solved by police even in a cooperative and civil relationship with the citizenry."[27] Some of the causes of crime are clearly beyond police control, including poverty, broken families, and unemployment.[28] These intractable factors cannot be controlled by the police; all the police can do is focus on the factors that they have some ability to control—even if they are the factors that are not the most highly correlated with crime.[29] However, it is not necessary to know the specific causes of crime in order to reduce it. The focus of police administrators should be on allocating and deploying officers to efficiently and effectively manage and reduce crime.

While the fundamental ability of the police to control or affect crime is still debated in some circles, there are a variety of specific patrol deployment strategies that have been shown to be effective:

- Offender-specific strategies that focus on serious and repeat offenders have been effective in specific deterrence;[30]
- Place-specific strategies, in particular "hot-spot" strategies, have been particularly effective in reducing calls for service and repeat victimization at a small number of addresses;[31] and
- Offense-specific strategies that focus on a particular offense or category of offenses have also been shown to be effective.[32]

For example, patrol deployment tactics emphasizing weapons seizures in Kansas City were found to have significantly reduced gun crime, drive-by shootings, homicides, and citizen fear of crime.[33] Similar findings were observed in a gun violence reduction project in Indianapolis.[34] In Indianapolis, significant violence reduction resulted from a directed patrol project, and the project also improved citizen satisfaction with the police.

Overall, Repetto found that the way officers are trained, deployed, and managed has a substantial, if not primary, impact on police productivity.[35] A number of organizational variables including deployment, call response patterns, specific patrol activities, and supervisory and training practices were all found to impact the efficiency and effectiveness of patrol.[36]

The result of the police research that was conducted during the 1970s led to the conclusion that nondirective patrol is not a legitimate crime control practice.[37] A proactive deployment plan must be developed based on attainable goals and reasonable objectives. This philosophy assumes that crime prevention is not attainable through the use of "sit around and wait" patrol. Rather, the primary emphasis must be on the repression and suppression of crime through innovative and proactive deployment tactics.[38] Measuring the effectiveness of patrol is fraught with difficulty, the least of which is measuring exactly how many crimes are deterred. Very few crime prevention programs (especially patrol programs) have been evaluated using scientifically recognized standards and methodologies including repeated tests under similar and differing social conditions.[39] One meta-analysis revealed that, based on a review of over 500 prevention program evaluations meeting minimum scientific standards, there was minimal evidence to establish what works, what doesn't, and what is promising in policing.[40]

RECENT DEPLOYMENT STRATEGIES AND TACTICS

In terms of deployment procedure, the Kansas City Preventive Patrol Experiment clearly indicated that uncommitted patrol time would be better spent on activities other than random preventive patrol. This study and others suggested that resources could be safely shifted away from preventive patrol and that as much as 50 percent of uncommitted time could be spent elsewhere. As a result, more directed patrol methods, using tactics targeted to address specific problems, became increasingly popular. Subsequent research and innovation has advanced our understanding of what works in policing.[41] However, there is still a lack of authoritative knowledge about which specific tactics work best against what types of problems in what kinds of settings.[42]

Obviously, numerous variations of tactical deployment of patrol resources are possible. Directed assignments could include short-term tactics intended to raise the perception of risk of apprehension. These might include saturation patrol, increased field interrogations, increased traffic enforcement, and other "aggressive" patrol procedures causing increased or high visibility. Directed patrol is attractive to police managers for at least two reasons. First, directed patrol addresses the primary criticism associated with random patrol because it focuses patrol resources on particular suspects, crimes, and/or target areas. Second, the strategy is neither officer-directed nor community-directed, but rather information-directed and management-directed. Traditionally, calls for service have dictated the deployment of a substantial portion of patrol resources, and the use of the remainder of patrol officer time has been left to individual discretion. Tactical patrol strategies are a means for police managers to regain some control over their most significant resource; the time and activities of patrol officers. Careful implementation and evaluation are essential, though, if the goals of tactical patrol are to be reached and its potential benefits realized.[43]

There are several patrol deployment strategies and tactics that have received attention in the literature in recent years. Numerous labels have been attached to a wide variety of programs implemented in departments across the nation. Many of these strategies and tactics will be discussed in greater detail in Chapters 6 and 7 but briefly, they include the following:

- *Order Maintenance Policing* The assumption in order maintenance policing is that focusing on less serious disorder offenses will lead to a decrease in more serious forms of crime. The "broken windows" theory developed by Wilson and Kelling serves as a theoretical basis.[44]
- *Crime Analysis and Patrol* Crime analysis units are probably the least understood and most misused units in many police departments. Although crime analysis is not a deployment strategy or tactic, its role in patrol cannot be understated. Crime analysis attempts to identify patterns in criminal offenses and calls for service within a department. This information is then given to patrol commanders to provide focus for the patrol shift and officers. Crime analysis is a central part of several of the strategies discussed in this section.
- *Problem-Oriented Policing* Problem-oriented policing or POP has served as a philosophical foundation for several deployment tactics. The idea is that calls for service and crime are caused by an underlying problem. The goal of the police, therefore, is to identify the underlying problem and solve it which will lead to reductions in crime and calls for service.
- *Aggressive Patrol and Crackdowns* Officers on patrol aggressively enforce the criminal law stopping every law violator. A crackdown can be for a single crime (e.g., drunk driving or prostitution), a variety of crimes (e.g., traffic offenses or vice), or focus on a specific type of offender (e.g., gangs or drug dealers). The tactic is to arrest as many people as possible through aggressive patrol and enforcement of the law.
- *Split-Force* Split-force patrol "splits" or "divides" the patrol force into two distinct and separate functions. One part of the patrol force is assigned to respond to calls for service, investigate crimes, and perform other assigned apprehension duties. Another part of the patrol force is held in reserve for the express purpose of conducting preventive patrol, or as a deterrent agent. The idea

is that by splitting the force, one can more effectively deploy resources and do a better job at utilizing patrol time.

- **High Visibility Patrol**   High visibility patrol is intended to increase the visible presence of police officers in an area. This can be accomplished through a variety of means. This tactic may or may not involve making additional arrests or aggressively enforcing the law. The assumption is that the mere presence or omnipresence of the police in an area is enough to deter crime.

- **Saturation Patrol**   The goal of saturation patrol is to place a substantially greater number of police personnel in an area or "saturate" an area with coverage. The officers may engage in a variety of tactics including simply being additional units responding to calls for service. The actual level of saturation or number of additional units required to saturate an area has not been consistently defined.

- **Directed Patrol**   Officers on directed patrol are given information regarding target selection, patrol tactics, and other procedures to follow while on patrol—they are "directed" as to how to spend their time and their energy. The assumption is that simply driving around or waiting for crime to occur is not effective and it is possible through crime analysis to select specific targets for increased surveillance or direct specific tactics designed to apprehend criminals or prevent crime.

- **Foot Patrol**   Foot patrol has received increased attention in recent years with the advent of COP. The idea is that putting officers into patrol cars has separated them from the community and thus created a disjuncture between the police and the community. The goal of the new foot patrol is to reacquaint the police with the community thus providing the community with increased feelings of safety and satisfaction.

- **Hot Spots**   Hot spots is a tactic similar to directed patrol that focuses on areas within a community or beat that generate a disproportionate amount of calls for service. The idea is that a small number of addresses or places are responsible for the majority of calls for service and crime in an area, and if police agencies focus resources on these areas, then calls for service and crime can be reduced.

- **Differential Police Response**   Differential police response strategies are designed to increase the efficiency and effectiveness of patrol allocation. This is accomplished by differentiating systematically among requests for service, and varying who responds, in what form, and with what rapidity in accordance with a priority system established by department policy.

None of these strategies exists in a vacuum, nor are they mutually exclusive. Innovative patrol programs typically combine a variety of the deployment strategies and tactics that are reviewed here. Therefore, it is incumbent on police administrators to decide what strategies and tactics will be used in allocating and deploying patrol resources in their jurisdictions.

The research and literature reviewed in this chapter underscores several problems that currently exist regarding patrol research. "Traditional police thinking about crime has put the cart before the horse: It has tried to make crime problems respond to police strategies, rather than crafting strategies to fit the crime problems."[44] Reducing opportunities for criminal access to vulnerable places, people, and things is probably far more important for preventing crime and should be a major factor in constructing specific police deployment strategies for specific crime problems. Only recently, researchers and police administrators have implemented the "crime-specific" philosophy suggested subsequent to the Kansas City Preventive Patrol Study. Only as a result of federal and foundation funding was scientific diagnosis, theory-building and experimentation brought to bear on police strategies for fighting crime. Even then, however, the research and testing was driven by basic strategies rather than by diagnosis of the problems. The focus on strategies rather than specific problems produced a misguided reform agenda. Rather than trying new and different strategies intended to fight crime, police reformers devoted most of their energy to altering the inputs for those strategies. Administrators and researchers have often blamed the failure of patrol and investigations on poorly trained police officers, inadequately trained police managers, inflexible civil service systems, weak disciplinary controls, and political interference.[45]

Sherman and Weisburd cite the results of the Minneapolis Hot Spots research in their conclusion regarding the efficacy of patrol, "(hot spots) offers a more powerful and more externally valid test of the patrol deterrence hypothesis than the Kansas City experiment. At the very least, it is time for criminologists to stop saying 'there is no evidence' that police patrol can affect crime."[46] So where are we at this point? First, the effectiveness of patrol is still largely undetermined and under-researched when viewed in relation to the resources allocated to patrol divisions. The police still patrol, but patrol allocation and deployment is still based on concepts and theories long since discarded. Second, there is a need for additional research on the best way to optimize patrol service delivery and allocation. Current practices are haphazard and largely a function of the innovation or lack thereof of local officials. Finally, several goals of police patrol are still salient and are still being pursued by police agencies. These goals, as we saw earlier, include crime prevention, responding to calls for service, rapid response to certain types of calls for service, visibility in the community, and geographic coverage for immediate availability. The questions of how many patrol officers, when, where, and what purpose they should serve continue to perplex many police researchers and practitioners.

ENDNOTES

1. G. W. Cordner and D. C. Hale, *What Works in Policing?* (Cincinnati, Ohio: Anderson Publishing, 1992); S. Walker and C. M. Katz, *Police in America: An Introduction*, 5th ed. (New York: McGraw-Hill, 2005).

2. S. Walker, *The Police in America* (New York: McGraw-Hill, 1992).

3. Walker and Katz, *Police in America*; R. A. Weisheit, D. N. Falcone, and L. E. Wells, *Crime and Policing in Rural and Small-Town America* (Prospect Heights, IL: Waveland Press, 1996).

4. L. W. Sherman and R. A. Berk, "The Specific Deterrent Effects of Arrest for Domestic Assault," *American Sociological Review* 49, no. 2 (1984): 261–72.

5. F. W. Dunford, D. Huizinga, and D. S. Elliot, "The Role of Arrest in Domestic Assault: The Omaha Police Experiment," *Criminology* 28 (1990): 183–206.

6. J. Skolnick and D. Bayley, *The New Blue Line: Police Innovation in Six American Cities* (New York, N.Y.: Free Press, 1986), 4–5.

7. Ibid.

8. T. Baker, R. R. Hunter, and J. P. Rush, *Police Systems and Practices: An Introduction* (Upper Saddle River, N.J.: Prentice Hall Career & Technology, 1994); N. Cameron, "The Police and Crime Control: Effectiveness, Community Policing, and Legal Change," *Criminal Law Forum* 1, no. 3 (1990): 477–512; G. L. Kelling, *What Works—Research and the Police* (Washington, D.C.: National Institute of Justice, 1988); C. Klockars, "Order Maintenance, The Quality of Urban Life and Police: A Different Line of Argument," in *Police Leadership in America: Crisis and Opportunity*, ed. W. A. Geller (New York, N.Y.: Praeger, 1986), 309–21; R. Trojanowicz and B. Bucqueroux, *Community Policing: A*

Contemporary Perspective (Cincinnati, Ohio: Anderson, 1990).

9. V. G. Strecher, *Goal Oriented Policing: Major Police Studies and Findings*. Unpublished Manuscript (Huntsville, Tex.: Sam Houston State University, 1993), 1.

10. Skolnick and Bayley, *The New Blue Line: Police Innovation in Six American Cities*.

11. L. W. Sherman, "Police Crackdowns: Initial and Residual Deterrence," in *Crime and Justice: An Annual Review of Research*, Vol. 12, ed. M. Tonry and N. Morris (Chicago, IL: University of Chicago Press, 1990), 1–48.

12. P. Manning, *Police Work: The Social Organization of Policing* (Cambridge, Mass.: MIT Press, 1977).

13. W. G. Gay, T. H. Schell, and S. Schack, *Improving Patrol Productivity: Volume I- Routine Patrol* (Washington, D.C.: U.S. Government Printing Office, 1977).

14. G. L. Kelling, *Foot Patrol* (Washington, D.C.: National Institute of Justice, 1985), 1.

15. O. W. Wilson, *Police Planning*, 2nd ed. (Springfield, IL: Charles C. Thomas, 1957).

16. K. O. Thompson, *Proactive Patrol—Is It of Value in the Prevention or Control of Crime?: An Evaluation of Proactive Patrol in Preventive Policing—The New Zealand Experience* (Hampshire, UK: Police College, Basingstoke, 1976).

17. R. C. Larson and M. F. Cahn, *Synthesizing and Extending the Results of Police Patrol Studies* (Washington, D.C.: National Institute of Justice, 1981).

18. M. S. Meagher, "Police Patrol Styles: How Pervasive Is Community Variation?" *Journal of Police Science and Administration* 13, no. 1 (1985): 36–45.

19. L. W. Sherman, "Police in the Laboratory of Criminal Justice," in *Critical Issues in Policing Contemporary*

Readings, ed. R. G. Dunham and G. P. Alpert (Prospect Heights, IL: Waveland, 1983), 72–93.

20. Walker and Katz, *Police in America*.

21. Cordner and Hale, *What Works in Policing?*

22. A. Reiss, *The Police and the Public* (New Haven, Conn.: Yale University Press, 1976).

23. Walker and Katz, *Police in America*.

24. C. N. Famega, "Variation in Officer Downtime: A Review of the Research," *Policing: An International Journal of Police Strategies and Management* 28, no. 3 (2005): 388–414; G. P. Whittaker, "What Is Patrol Work?" *Police Studies* 4, no. 4 (1982): 13–22.

25. G. L. Kelling, "Defining the Bottom Line in Policing: Organizational Philosophy and Accountability," in *Quantifying Quality in Policing*, ed. L. T. Hoover (Washington, D.C.: Police Executive Research Forum, 1996), 31.

26. L. T. Hoover and T. J. Caeti, "Crime Specific Policing in Houston," *Texas Law Enforcement Management and Administrative Statistics Program Bulletin* 1, no. 9 (1994): 1–12.

27. G. L. Kelling and D. Fogel, "Police Patrol—Some Future Directions," in *The Future of Policing*, ed. A. W. Cohn (Beverly Hills, CA.: Sage, 1978), 177.

28. L. W. Sherman, "Patrol Strategies for Police," in *Crime and Public Policy*, ed. J. Q. Wilson (San Francisco, CA: ICS Press, 1983b), 145–63.

29. Sherman, *Critical Issues in Policing Contemporary Readings*.

30. L. W. Sherman, "Attacking Crime: Police and Crime Control," in *Crime and Justice: A Review of Research,* Vol. 15, ed. M. Tonry and N. Morris (Chicago, IL: University of Chicago Press, 1992), 159–230; A. F. Abrahamse, P. A. Ebener, P. W. Greenwood, N. Fitzgerald, and T. E. Kosin, "An Experimental Evaluation of the Phoenix Repeat Offender Program," *Justice Quarterly* 8, no. 2 (1991): 141–69; S. E. Martin, "Policing Career Criminals: An Examination of an Innovative Crime Control Program," *The Journal of Criminal Law and Criminology* 77, no. 4 (1986): 1159–182; S. E. Martin and L. W. Sherman, "Catching Career Criminals: Proactive Policing and Selective Apprehension," *Justice Quarterly* 3, no. 2 (1986): 171–92.

31. Sherman, *Crime and Justice: An Annual Review of Research*; *Crime and Justice A Review of Research*; A. A. Braga, "Research Findings from Prevention and Intervention Studies: The Effects of Hot Spots Policing on Crime," *The Annals of the American Academy of Political and Social Science* 578, no. 1 (2001): 104–25.

32. Sherman, *Crime and Justice: An Annual Review of Research*; *Crime and Justice A Review of Research*; L. W. Sherman and D. P. Rogan, "Effects of Gun Seizures on Gun Violence: 'Hot Spots' Patrol in Kansas City," *Justice Quarterly* 12, no. 4 (1995): 673–93.

33. Sherman and Rogan, "Effects of Gun Seizures on Gun Violence."

34. E. F. McGarrel, S. Chermak, and A. Weiss, *Reducing Gun Violence: Evaluation of the Indianapolis Police Department's Directed Patrol Project* (Washington, D.C.: National Institute of Justice, 2002).

35. T. A. Reppetto, "The Influence of Police Organizational Style on Crime Control Effectiveness," *Journal of Police Science and Administration* 3, no. 3 (1975): 274–79.

36. Ibid.

37. J. H. Auten, "Crime Prevention and Police Patrol—Are They Compatible?" *Police Chief* 48, no. 8 (1981): 60–67; A. M. Newton, "Prevention of Crime and Delinquency," *Criminal Justice Abstracts* 10, no. 2 (1978): 245–66.

38. Auten, *Police Chief*.

39. L. W. Sherman, D. C. Gottfredson, D. L. MacKenzie, J. Eck, P. Reuter, and S. D. Bushway, *Preventing Crime: What Works, What Doesn't, What's Promising* (Washington, D.C.: National Institute of Justice, 1998).

40. Ibid.

41. Cordner and Hale, *What Works in Policing?*

42. G. W. Cordner and D. J. Kenney, "Tactical Patrol Evaluation," in *Police Program Evaluation*, ed. L. T. Hoover (Washington, D.C.: Police Executive Research Forum, 1998), 15–55.

43. Ibid.

44. Sherman, *Crime and Public Policy*, 72.

45. Sherman, *Critical Issues in Policing Contemporary Readings*; *Crime and Public Policy*.

46. L. W. Sherman and D. Weisburd, "General Deterrent Effects of Police Patrol in Crime 'Hot Spots': A Randomized, Controlled Trial," *Justice Quarterly* 12, no. 4 (1995): 647.

Patrol Allocation

CHAPTER

3

Historical Analysis of Patrol Allocation and Deployment Models

The question, "How many officers should be assigned to patrol?" is simple to ask but difficult to answer. Several models have been developed over the past 50 years to try to answer the above question. Allocation models for police patrol seek to determine how many officers need to be assigned to patrol in order to provide the level of service needed in a community. If an agency has a force of 1,000 sworn officers, an allocation model can estimate how many of those 1,000 officers need to be assigned to patrol to meet the objectives of the department. Allocation models need to be distinguished from deployment models however. Deployment models answer the questions "where?" and "when?", while allocation models answer the question "how many?". In other words, while allocation models for police patrol determine how many officers should be assigned to the patrol function, deployment models determine where the officers should be assigned (e.g., which district or sector, which beats, which responsibilities, etc.) and when they should be assigned (i.e., day of week and time of day). For example, a deployment model can help an administrator determine how many officers should be assigned to a particular division on a particular day of the week and a particular time of the day. This is not the function of an allocation model. Although this distinction is prevalent today, some of the models discussed in this chapter serve as both allocation and deployment models. However, they are typically referred to as allocation models because the early models used the term allocation and deployment synonymously. This chapter provides a comprehensive historical analysis of patrol allocation and deployment models along with their limitations.

EARLY POLICE PATROL ALLOCATION MODELS

August Vollmer developed a list of police functions, many of which still persist today.[1] Among the items on the list were crime prevention, crime suppression, criminal apprehension, criminal investigation, public service, order maintenance, traffic control, and emergency services. Vollmer was the first to develop a territorial subunit, namely the beat, as a means to more efficiently allocate police resources. He suggested that police should be allocated and beats should be constructed based on a workload analysis and calls for service.[2] He also suggested that the police develop their craft into a profession based on technical competence that would effectively utilize technological developments to better police the community they served. Some of the ideas and problems recognized in the early professionalization movement still exist today. Early police theorists argued that patrol allocation must be altered in response to changing political, socioeconomic, and crime problems in communities. Further, the use of crime analysis to determine the best formula to allocate police patrol resources was advanced. Several police theorists recognized that patrol units and personnel were traditionally allocated equally throughout the day and without regard to crime patterns or calls for service.[3] This early work led to some departments allocating patrol units based on workload; however, some departments still allocate patrol resources evenly to this day.

During the 1960s and 1970s, operations research elaborated on the preventive patrol model, and the Law Enforcement Assistance Administration (LEAA) allocated significant funds for the development of technology and hardware to improve patrol including complex patrol allocation models, computer-aided dispatch (CAD), and vehicle locator systems.[4] In addition, complex computer software and mathematical models were developed to maximize the randomness and increase the omnipresence of the police on patrol. Operations researchers, engineers, economists, and mathematicians became interested in police patrol in the late 1960s and early 1970s and developed several different formulas and methods for the allocation and deployment of patrol resources.[5] By the time the Kansas City Preventive Patrol Experiment had begun, departments across the country had adopted a variety of patrol workload and analysis methods. All of these attempted to take into account a variety of factors thought to be related to patrol effectiveness. Generally, the factors were the level and distribution of manpower, the shift hours, and the size and configuration of patrol beats.[6] All of the models assumed that the police, through simple presence and optimal coverage, could deter and control crime.

Allocation by Geography

Many of the earliest patrol allocation models were based on allocation by geography. In allocation by geography, patrol units are deployed based on the percentage of square miles in the total area to be patrolled.[7] Allocation by geography generally meant that equal numbers of patrol units were distributed based on patrol beats. Further, equal numbers of units would staff the beats on each of the three shifts, regardless of demand. By the 1960s, many in law enforcement were developing systems that attempted to move away from equal staffing and allocation by geography to models based on demand.[8] These innovations were hailed as groundbreaking and served as a source of pride for the departments that implemented them.[9] The apex of the research into allocation by geography was the development of the hypercube model, which mathematically assisted in the design of patrol beats.[10]

Allocation by Hazard Formula

The original hazard formula was developed by O. W. Wilson in the 1940s and was still widely in use prior to the Kansas City Preventive Patrol Experiment. Wilson formulated a deployment scheme based on allocation by hazard that was first implemented in the Los Angeles Police Department in 1953. Each type of crime was given a weighted hazard score and, by prioritizing the incidence of crime, a total weighted sum for each region was calculated with personnel being allocated accordingly.[11] The formula as developed by Wilson, with minor refinements, was still in use in the 1980s.[12] The weighting criteria and factors were totally subjective in nature, yet many police managers insisted that over time, the factors were refined to an accurate number. The primary problem with the hazard model was that the number of arrests made in the preceding period in a given area could be due to an over allocation of units, thereby generating an even higher allocation of units in the following period. A method to improve the selection of the subjective ratings was never developed or published.[13] The hazard model emphasized the redistribution of patrol forces based on a set of proportionate need factors, which were based on the particular crimes that represented the highest police demands.[14] The weightings were not perfect, but the assignment of weights according to classes of events was the best available at the time.[15] The hazard models began to come under criticism because of several shortcomings including faulty math and because the system did not offer a mechanism to study or assess policy relevant variables.[16]

Allocation by Queuing Models

Queuing models attempted to overcome the problem of subjectiveness of allocation by geography and hazard formula models. Queuing models combined probabilistic demands for service with geographic considerations in an effort to reduce the amount of time in responding to urgent calls for service.[17] In 1964, an advanced queuing model was developed and implemented in the St. Louis, Missouri Police Department.[18] The model combined prediction by exponential smoothing with assignment of response cars by queuing. The St. Louis model was based on the demand for police services predicted by hour and geographic area, using projections based on past demand data with modifications for weekly and seasonal variations. The exponential smoothing took into account the variations in calls for service by time of day, day of week, week of year, and overall trends in the rate of calls for service. In effect, the exponential smoothing purported to estimate future calls for service by averaging the volumes of calls experienced in the past, with the most recent data being given the most weight.[19] The result was an estimate, down to the hour, of calls for service in a given area.

The prediction model asserted that manpower could be distributed on the basis of urgent calls having to wait in delay for a specific length of time before being serviced, hence the namesake "queuing delay."[20] St. Louis allocated personnel based on the probability that, at most, 15 percent of each district's calls will be delayed in queue, thus, more resources could be allocated to areas with the highest queue time. Queuing models were the first attempt to apply mathematical and probability modeling to police patrol allocation. In theory, the model appears to be adaptable to changes in crime patterns within particular jurisdictions, however a number of problems with the model were eventually identified.[21]

First, no attempt was made to structure or take into account uncommitted patrol time. In fact, uncommitted time was averaged into weekly estimates for demand resulting in delays higher than estimated or predicted at certain times of the day.[22] Second, the method utilized only one criterion for deployment, the fraction of calls that could not be immediately answered by a patrol unit. In other words, the model assumed that weekly demand followed a typical pattern over the hours of the week without controlling for time or location. As one researcher noted, techniques that average or estimate general predictions about police workload and the total number of calls for service in a city are simply "not very helpful in the day-to-day deployment of police officers."[23] Third, the model did not distinguish between a high priority call and a low priority call—a robbery in progress conceivably carried the same weight as a traffic accident and was just as likely to be queued (delayed). Finally, the model was influenced by rapid changes in calls-for-service patterns. As such, allocation could be rapidly increased, but only in the week after the rise in calls was observed. In this sense, it was entirely reactive which would lead to an over-deployment of patrol resources after a "crisis" situation was already over.

An adaptation of the queuing model was offered by IBM in the form of the Law Enforcement Manpower Resource Allocation System (LEMRAS). LEMRAS was essentially the queuing system with an additional mechanism for prioritizing calls based on the need for a more rapid response.[24] Elements of LEMRAS can still be seen in some CAD systems, which prioritize calls for service. However, LEMRAS, since it was built on the queuing model, also suffered from the same problems.[25]

Allocation for the Prevention of Crime

In 1967, the Science and Technology Task Force of the President's Commission on Law Enforcement and Administration of Justice recommended that police operations should be analyzed and recast to reflect more quantitative and sophisticated methods.[26] As a result of this charge, several mathematical models were developed to attempt to maximize the suppression of crime through preventive patrol. These models attempted to identify the probability of intercepting a crime in progress and the probability of a crime taking place. Subsequent to substantial and complex mathematical calculations, the amount of patrol needed to satisfy a minimal level of apprehension could be calculated.[27] The most well-publicized methods were the simulation and travel-time models.

Richard Larson from MIT developed such a model that built on the work of the hazard and queuing models. The simulation model, he developed, allocated patrol resources based largely on travel time. The model prioritized the expected travel time to a call for service based on geography, the number of available patrol units, and the demand rates of calls for service. A heuristic programming algorithm was used to produce an optimal response time for certain areas. A simulation model was then generated to assess allocation and deployment tactics. The simulation model worked by examining where incidents were occurring in the city and then assigning a priority number to each incident (low numbers for high priority calls). As each call came in, an attempt was made to dispatch a patrol unit to the call, however not all calls were assigned immediately. Unassigned calls were placed in the queue which was depleted as units became available. The model was a sophisticated one and preferred over both the queuing and LEMRAS models in that it took into account the average length of travel to a call, the average amount of time a call took to clear, a range of dispatching priorities, and several other performance measures. Any variety of performance variables could be included in the algorithm.[28]

The simulation model suffered from several flaws, all of which are assumptional rather than mathematical. The model assumed that crime occurred randomly, that the probability of space–time coincidence of crime and patrol could be measured, and that crime occurrence and patrol were independent.[29] Future studies of crime patterns, directed patrol analysis, and random patrol's effect on crime would limit the utility of these models. As Pate, Kelling, and Brown note, "neither Larson's models nor his data are adequate to make statements about typical patrol intensities in major American cities."[30] Nonetheless, the variables that influenced these models continue to influence patrol allocation to this day.

Patrol Car Allocation Model

The Patrol Car Allocation Model (PCAM) is a computer program designed to assist and enable police departments to determine the number of patrol units to have on duty during various times of the day and days of the week.[31] The PCAM model can account for busy periods and is considered a priority system for calls in calculating the number of units needed.[32] It is based heavily on Larson's program, with substantial improvements. The program was developed jointly by the United States Department of Justice and Housing and Urban Development in 1975. Its capabilities are described in the user manual written by Chaiken and Dormant.[33]

PCAM is a simple analytic model. It provides two patrol performance objectives—dispatch delay and response time. For this reason, it is frequently referred to as a performance-oriented system. PCAM is significantly different from previous models, discussed above, in that it does not attempt to equalize the calls-for-service workload across watches or shifts. Instead, its goal is to deploy officers so that dispatch delays and response times (performance monitors) can be optimized.[34] PCAM has both descriptive and prescriptive capabilities. It is very flexible and can specify particular allocations that best meet the standards of performance established by individual users. When operated descriptively, an evaluation of current patrol allocation can be done against the user-set performance indicators. When operated prescriptively, the program will recommend the "best" temporal allocation of existing resources. The "best" allocation plan can be defined by setting parameters for geographical commands, different times of the day or week, average number of calls placed in queue, and the total dispatch and response time.[35]

Unlike the simulation model developed by Larson, PCAM is not based on a randomly-moving patrol car assumption, nor does it hold constant specific probability and gaming functions. It is almost entirely controlled by user input and user designation of performance monitors. The natural limitation is contained in the number and type of parameters available. For instance, the model reflects no geographical structure and is insensitive to the locations of patrol cars within a specific area. Also, differences in crime rates, call-for-service trends, and patrol densities are not easily augmented to the program. For this reason, continual updating requires the user to write subsidiary computer programs; a costly and time-consuming procedure. Further, PCAM fails to allow dispatching patrol cars across command boundaries for high-priority calls; a procedure which is quite common and many times imperative in police deployment plans.[36]

PCAM has three basic prescriptive capabilities. The first is to determine the minimum number of patrol units that must be on duty in each geographical area during all hours of the day in order to meet performance objectives related to one or more of the data items specified.[37] The data items can include the following:

- Average workload of patrol units;
- Average amount of uncommitted time for patrol units;
- Average travel time to incidents;
- Percentage of calls that will have to wait in queue until a patrol unit is available to dispatch to the incident;
- Average number of minutes a call in each priority class will have to wait in queue;

- Average patrol frequency; and
- Average total response time (time in queue plus travel time).[38]

The second capability of PCAM is to determine the best allocation across sectors and/or among different times of the day or week based on optimization of: (1) the smallest possible percentage of calls that must be placed in queue; (2) the smallest possible average length of time calls for a given priority must wait in queue; or (3) the smallest possible average total response time.[39] Finally, PCAM's third prescriptive capability combines the first two and allows the user to develop an allocation plan that best fits the objectives in mind.[40]

In 1978, the Law Enforcement Assistance Administration tested the PCAM model in three sites: Albuquerque, New Mexico; Charlotte, North Carolina; and Sacramento, California. Unfortunately, an experimental design was precluded prior to assessment because of several difficulties.[41] Further, the model was not tested exclusively—it was combined with a variety of other initiatives designed to "direct" patrol activities. This funding and site assessment was undertaken as a direct result of the research findings of the 1970s.

SUMMARY OF EARLY ALLOCATION METHODS

The majority of models used in patrol allocation were developed prior to 1980. These models can be divided into five categories: allocation by geography, allocation by hazard formula, allocation by queuing, allocation for the prevention of crime, and the PCAM. The models vary in complexity. As allocation models for patrol evolved, they became much more sophisticated and complex, taking into account numerous variables that impact allocation and performing complex mathematical calculations in determining the number of officers that need to be assigned to patrol.

In allocation by geography, patrol units are deployed simply based on the percentage of square miles in the total area to be patrolled.[42] Allocation by geography generally meant that equal numbers of patrol units were distributed based on patrol beats. Further, equal numbers of units were deployed on each of the three shifts, regardless of demand.[43] In allocation by hazard formula, sophistication increased with each type of crime being given a weighted hazard score and, by prioritizing the incidence of crime, a total weighted sum for each district was calculated with personnel being allocated accordingly.[44]

Allocation by queuing models attempted to overcome the subjectiveness of geographic and hazard models. Queuing models combine probabilistic demands for service with geographical considerations in an effort to reduce the amount of time in responding to urgent calls for service.[45] The models assert that officers should be distributed on the basis of urgent calls having to wait in delay for a specific length of time before being serviced. Queuing models were the first attempt to apply mathematical and probability modeling to patrol allocation.

Allocation for the prevention of crime includes several mathematical computations that were developed to attempt to maximize the suppression of crime through preventive patrol. These models attempted to identify the probability of intercepting a crime in progress and the probability of a crime taking place. After several complex mathematical calculations the amount of patrol needed to satisfy a minimal level of apprehension could be calculated.[46]

Larson's model built on the work of the hazard and queuing models. The model, he developed, allocated officers based largely on geography, the number of available patrol units, and the demand rates of calls for service.[47] The formulas used in such a model are quite complex. For example, the formula used to determine the average number of on-duty officers required per day to meet a response time objective for non-emergency activities is:

$$N_{\text{nett}} = \left[\frac{40}{\text{PTT} \times \text{RS}} \right]^2 \times \frac{A \times \text{WC}}{7 \times S_1}$$

where

N_{nett} = average number of on-duty officers required per day to meet a response time objective for non-emergency activities,

A = area (square miles) of the patrol district,

WC = coverage (hours) per week,

PTT = average response time objective (minutes) for non-emergency activities,

RS = average response speed (mph),

S_1 = shift length (hours).[48]

The formula is based on the "square root law," which can be used to estimate the average travel distance for a responding police unit in an area of a particular size with a particular number of available units and is just one of numerous complex formulas used in allocation models for patrol.[49] Models developed since Larson's allocation for the prevention of crime model are even more mathematically complex.

The PCAM is a computer program designed to enable departments to determine the number of patrol units to have on duty during various times of the day. PCAM is based heavily on Larson's allocation for the prevention of crime model, with substantial improvements. PCAM takes into account two patrol performance objectives: dispatch delay and response time. For this reason, it is frequently referred to as a performance-oriented system. By utilizing PCAM, the best allocation plan can be determined by setting parameters for geographical commands, different times of the day or week, average number of calls placed in queue, and the total dispatch and response time.[50]

One of the pronounced shortcomings of early police patrol allocation models is that none of these were systematically validated. For the most part, the evaluation of patrol deployment plans has not been well developed and has failed to make use of experimental designs.[51] Very few of the designs were ever fully implemented to measure what the police actually did.[52] Instead, they attempted to measure the effect of increased or decreased response times, elapsed times, police presence, workload, calls for service, etc. As a result, no definitive statements can be made about the effectiveness of the early models described. Any attempt or desire to analyze these models was reduced by the results and subsequent debate surrounding the Kansas City Preventive Patrol Experiment and other prominent police research of the 1970s. Today, even though many police departments are still using the deployment and allocation formulas just described, there is no systematic empirical research concerning their effectiveness.[53] In fact, many departments still deploy by geography, assigning one officer per beat without regard to calls for service or crime patterns.

MODERN POLICE PATROL ALLOCATION MODELS

The previous discussion notes that each generation of allocation model builds upon earlier models and, as these models evolve, they become more complex. For example, early queuing models utilized only one basic criterion for allocation, those fractions of calls that could not be immediately answered by a patrol unit. The next generation of allocation models dealt with the prevention of crime. These models were more sophisticated and preferred over queuing models in that they took into account several variables in determining allocation needs including the average length of travel to a call, the average amount of time a call takes to clear, a range of dispatching priorities, and several other performance measures. Larson developed such a model.[54] PCAM built upon Larson's model and focused on two patrol performance objectives: dispatch delay and response time.

Little work was done on allocation models in the 1980s, but the next generation was introduced in 1993. Supported by National Highway Traffic Safety Administration funding, Northwestern University's Traffic Institute developed the Patrol Allocation Model (PAM). Computerized and elaborated versions of PAM represent the current state of the art of patrol allocation.

In developing the PAM model, the Traffic Institute field tested the model in the following 12 cities:

- Boise (Idaho) Police Department
- Knoxville (Tennessee) Police Department
- Tucson (Arizona) Police Department
- Addison (Illinois) Police Department
- Boca Raton (Florida) Police Department
- Brick (New Jersey) Police Department

- Brunswick (Ohio) Police Department
- Chandler (Arizona) Police Department
- Crystal (Illinois) Police Department
- Medina (Ohio) Police Department
- Oak Park (Illinois) Police Department
- Sandy (Utah) Police Department

The PAM model is designed to determine the number of officers that need to be assigned to patrol based on established performance objectives. These performance objectives include visibility of officers, response time objectives for priority 1 and 2 calls for service, and immediate availability to respond to a priority 1 call for service. This model builds upon previous allocation models to take into account numerous variables that impact allocation of police patrol. Unfortunately, however, the model was created as a "paper and pencil" worksheet, which was time consuming to originally develop for a police department and prohibitive to making changes once the model was developed.

A more recent allocation model is the Allocation Model for Police Patrol (AMPP). This model was developed in 2001 by the authors of this text and expanded upon and extended the capabilities of the PAM model. When the AMPP model was created, several modifications were made to the original PAM model. First, several variables were added to the model. The AMPP model takes into account many variables that were not originally accounted for in the original PAM. Second, the model was computerized. As noted, the original PAM was a pencil and paper model. It was quite laborious to figure out the number of officers that needed to be assigned to patrol. Several worksheets and calculations needed to be completed, each by hand, and any modifications to the variables required recalculation of the entire model. Therefore, the model was not very user friendly. The AMPP model is computerized (employing Microsoft Excel®), and thus any changes to the values of the variables automatically leads to a recalculation of the bottom line; the number of officers that need to be assigned to patrol.

The latest patrol allocation model, the Model for the Allocation of Patrol Personnel (MAPP), was also developed by the authors of this text. It expands and extends the capabilities and functionality of the PAM and AMPP models discussed above. The MAPP is a comprehensive, *web-based* patrol allocation model centering around determining the number of patrol officers that need to be assigned to patrol in order to accomplish six performance objectives:

- Answering calls for service;
- Meeting response time goals;
- Optimizing visibility in the community;
- Having an officer available to immediately respond to an emergency;

- Providing officers ample time to perform self-initiated activities; and
- Allowing officers sufficient time to perform administrative activities.

Many agencies struggle to justify to budget committees and governing bodies the need for additional police patrol personnel. It is difficult for many agencies to quantify specifically what will be gained by adding more officers. The MAPP provides agencies with the ability to specify what will be gained by adding additional patrol officers. The gain may include more time to perform self-initiated activities, lowering response times, increasing availability and visibility, or increasing agency performance on any of the objectives listed above. The model is developed based on a set of input values. Once the model is developed for an agency, the input values can be modified to determine the impact the changes have on needed patrol staffing levels.

LIMITATIONS OF MODERN PATROL ALLOCATION MODELS

Allocation models are not panaceas; they certainly have limitations. These limitations need to be kept in mind while assessing the number of officers that need to be assigned to patrol according to an allocation model. First, the number of officers that need to be assigned to patrol as identified by an allocation model is only as accurate as the data used in the model. If the data on number of calls for service, average service time, leave percentage and other data-driven variables are inaccurate, then the estimate of the number of officers needed for patrol will likewise be inaccurate.

Second, allocation models provide an estimate of the number of officers that should be assigned to patrol and should not be used in lieu of professional expertise on the part of police administrators, but instead, should be used in conjunction with professional expertise. In other words, administrators should use allocation models as a tool to determine how many officers should be assigned to patrol. If administrators know that other factors, besides the ones accounted for in a particular model, also impact patrol resources in their jurisdictions, then those factors should also be taken into account in determining how many officers should be assigned to patrol.

Third, the estimate provided by an allocation model of the number of officers that need to be assigned to patrol contains error partially because it does not take into account all variables that impact allocation in a particular jurisdiction. Allocation models may take into account several variables, but not every variable that impacts allocation can be accounted for in a patrol allocation model. This creates some errors in the estimate of the number of officers needed for patrol.

Another potential source of error occurs because of the need to estimate some data items in allocation models. For example, the values for some of the variables that impact allocation may not be available from the police department, especially variables related to patrol speed. Therefore, if an agency does not have data on patrol speed, the agency must use data from another agency or the average patrol speed from prior patrol allocation studies. This may lead to error in the estimate provided by an allocation model because the average patrol speed borrowed from another agency may not match the actual patrol speed within the agency.

Fourth, data used in allocation models, especially calls-for-service data, are typically previous year data. Therefore, the number of officers needed, as identified by an allocation model, is typically accurate for last year but may not be completely accurate for the current year because of increases in calls for service or other factors. This is one of the limitations in allocation models. However, it is recommended that allocation models can also be used to forecast patrol strength needs. This can be done by analyzing trends in calls for service, average service time per call, roadway mile additions, among other variables and determining the percent increase or decrease in these variables over the past 5 years. Then, the latest data available (which will always be 1 year behind patrol needs) can be multiplied by the percent change over the 5-year trends on the variables mentioned above to obtain an estimate of patrol strength needs in the future. It is important to forecast needs into the future so that officers can be hired and trained prior to their need. If they are not hired and trained before the need for patrol officers arises, then patrol will always be understaffed.

Fifth, a problem in using a mathematical model to calculate needed patrol resources is the fact that policing is a dynamic system. A dynamic system is one that adjusts to changes in the environment. In the case of the patrol function, officers will alter their behavior depending upon the call load. On a shift with a light call load, officers will tend to spend more time on calls, not to mention breaks and administrative duties at the police station. On shifts where calls are in queue, and particularly when critical calls are backing up, officers under such circumstances will cut short their time at the police station, take fewer breaks, and even skip a lunch break. More importantly, they will reduce the amount of time spent on individual calls. Arguably, the quality of service may suffer when officers make such an adjustment, but at the same time they are being responsive to the need to get to other pending volatile situations quickly. Thus, any mathematical method that is designated as a simulation of such systems will be an estimate at best. Once again, however, it should be reiterated that a mathematical model that provides a reasonable estimate of patrol staffing levels given stipulated variations in service levels is far superior than mere guesswork.

ENDNOTES

1. G. E. Misner and R. Hoffman, *Police Resource Allocation* (Berkeley, CA: University of California Press, 1967).

2. A. Vollmer, "The Police Beat," in *Police Patrol Readings*, ed. S. G. Chapman (Springfield, IL: Charles C. Thomas, 1964).

3. F. E. Walton, "Selective Distribution of Police Patrol," in *Police Patrol Readings*, ed. S. G. Chapman (Springfield, IL: Charles C. Thomas, 1964).

4. J. Petersilia, "The Influence of Research on Policing," in *Critical Issues in Policing Contemporary Readings*, ed. R. G. Dunham and G. P. Alpert (Prospect Heights, IL: Waveland, 1993).

5. W. Bennett and J. DuBois, *The Use of Probability Theory in the Assignment of Police Patrol Areas* (Washington, D.C.: Government Printing Office, 1970); W. J. Brown and D. B. Butler, "Patrol Operations: Performance Measurement and Improvement," *Canadian Police Chief* 66, no. 3 (1977): 19–25, 36; G. L. Campbell, *A Spatially Distributed Queuing Model for Police Patrol Sector Design* (Cambridge, MA: MIT Press, 1972); C. Clawson, "Theoretical Approach to the Allocation of Police Preventive Patrol," *Police Chief* 40, no. 7 (1973): 53–59; J. A. Gylys, "Application of a Production Function to Police Patrol Activity," *Police Chief* 41, no. 7 (1974): 70–71; G. B. Hirsch and L. J. Riccio, "Measuring and Improving the Productivity of Police Patrol," *Journal of Police Science and Administration* 2, no. 2 (1974): 169–84; R. C. Larson, "On Quantitative Approaches to Urban Police Patrol Programs," *Journal of Research in Crime and Delinquency* 7, no. 2 (1970): 157–66; L. J. Riccio, "Direct Deterrence: An Analysis of the Effectiveness of Police Patrol and Other Crime Prevention Technologies," *Journal of Criminal Justice* 2, no. 3 (1974): 207–17.

6. D. A. Kelley and G. E. Fine, *Patrol Workload Study: A Procedure for the Allocation and Distribution of Patrol Manpower* (Sacramento, CA: California Commission on Peace Officer Standards and Training, 1974).

7. J. M. Chaiken and R. C. Larson, "Methods for Allocating Urban Emergency Units: A Survey," *Management Science* 19, December, 110–30; K. R. Chelst, *An Interactive Approach to Police Sector Design* (Cambridge, MA: MIT Press, 1974); S. B. Smith, *Superbeat: A System for the Effective Distribution of Police Patrol Units* (Chicago, IL: Illinois Institute of Technology, 1973).

8. C. J. Fisher and R. L. Smith, "Tampa Selective Deployment Patrol System," *Police Chief* 36, no. 6 (1969): 52–57.

9. Ibid; Smith, *Superbeat: A System for the Effective Distribution of Police Patrol Units*.

10. R. C. Larson, *Hypercube Queuing Model: Users Manual* (New York, NY: RAND Institute, 1975); R. C. Larson, "What Happened to Patrol Operations in Kansas City?" *Evaluation* 3, no. 1–2 (1976): 117–123.

11. O. W. Wilson, *Police Planning* (Springfield, IL: Charles C. Thomas, 1958).

12. R. W. Taylor, *An Analysis of Police Patrol Techniques*. Doctoral Diss., photocopied (Portland, OR: Portland State University, 1981).

13. Chaiken and Larson, "Methods for Allocating Urban Emergency Units"; T. J. Sweeney and W. Ellingsworth, eds, *Issues in Police Patrol—A Book of Readings* (Kansas City, MO: Kansas City Police Department, 1973).

14. Walton, *Police Patrol Readings*; Sweeney and Ellingsworth, *Issues in Police Patrol*.

15. D. T. Shanahan, *Patrol Administration: Management by Objectives* (Boston, MA: Allyn and Bacon, 1978).

16. Larson "On Quantitative Approaches to Urban Police Patrol Programs"; Sweeney and Ellingsworth, *Issues in Police Patrol.*

17. Chaiken and Larson, "Methods for Allocating Urban Emergency Units."

18. R. F. Crowther, *The Use of a Computer System for Police Manpower Allocation in St. Louis Missouri* (Terre Haute, IN: Indiana University, 1965); T. McEwan, *Allocation of Patrol Manpower Resources in the St. Louis Police Department* (St. Louis, MO: Metropolitan Police Department; Sweeney and Ellingsworth, 1966).

19. RAND Corporation, *Methods for Allocating Police Patrol Resources* (Santa Monica, CA: RAND Corporation, 1973); Sweeney and Ellingsworth, *Issues in Police Patrol.*

20. J. M. Chaiken, T. B. Crabill, L. P. Holliday, D. L. Jaquette, M. Lawless, and E. S. Quade, *Criminal Justice Models: An Overview* (Washington, D.C.: Government Printing Office, 1976).

21. Sweeney and Ellingsworth, *Issues in Police Patrol.*

22. Chaiken et al., *Criminal Justice Models.*

23. J. B. Richardson and R. Stout, "Incident Prediction Model for Police Placement," *Police Chief* 42, no. 4 (1975): 38.

24. Sweeney and Ellingsworth, *Issues in Police Patrol.*

25. RAND Corporation, *Methods for Allocating Police Patrol Resources.*

26. R. C. Larson, *Urban Police Patrol Analysis* (Cambridge, MA: MIT Press, 1972).

27. Chaiken and Larson, "Methods for Allocating Urban Emergency Units"; Larson, "On Quantitative Approaches to Urban Police Patrol Programs."

28. Larson, "On Quantitative Approaches to Urban Police Patrol Programs."

29. G. J. Sullivan, *Directed Patrol* (Kansas City, MO: Kansas City Police Department, 1976).

30. T. Pate, G. L. Kelling, and C. Brown, "Response to 'What Happened to Patrol Operations in Kansas City'", *Journal of Criminal Justice* 3, no. 4 (1975): 312.

31. W. G. Gay, T. H. Schell, and S. Schack, *Improving Patrol Productivity: Volume I-Routine Patrol* (Washington, D.C.: U.S. Government Printing Office, 1977).

32. M. J. Levine and T. J. McEwen, *Patrol Deployment* (Washington, D.C.: National Institute of Justice, 1985).

33. J. M. Chaiken and P. Dormant, *Patrol Car Allocation Method: Users Manual* (Santa Monica, CA: RAND Corporation, 1975).

34. Gay et al., *Improving Patrol Productivity.*

35. Ibid.

36. Chaiken et al., *Criminal Justice Models.*

37. A. Pasciuto, M. A. Beck, J. Bonner, W. Saulsbury, G. Silberman, and W. P. Travers, *Managing Patrol Operations: Program Test Design* (Washington, D.C.: National Institute of Justice, 1978).

38. Ibid.

39. Ibid.

40. Ibid.

41. Ibid.

42. Smith, *Superbeat.*

43. Fisher and Smith, "Tampa Selective Deployment Patrol System."

44. Wilson, *Police Planning.*

45. Chaiken and Larson, "Methods for Allocating Urban Emergency Units."

46. Ibid.

47. Larson, "On Quantitative Approaches to Urban Police Patrol Programs."

48. Traffic Institute, *Police Personnel Allocation Manual User's Guide* (Washington, D.C.: National Highway Traffic Safety Administration, 1993).

49. Ibid.

50. Gay et al., *Improving Patrol Productivity.*

51. J. Q. Wilson and B. Boland, "The Effect of the Police on Crime," *Law & Society* 12, no. 3 (1978): 367–90.

52. Ibid.

53. T. Ting-Jung, "Patrol Allocation," *Texas Law Enforcement Management and Administrative Statistics Program Bulletin* 2, no. 9 (1995): 1–8.

54. Larson, "On Quantitative Approaches to Urban Police Patrol Programs."

CHAPTER

4

Factors that Impact Patrol Allocation

INTRODUCTION

It is common for police administrators to ask some variation of the question, "How many patrol officers do we need?" In reality, there is no "right" answer to this question. How many police officers are needed depends upon what level of police services is desired. There is no fixed standard in this respect. Some communities want a priority 1 response time of 4 minutes; some are willing to tolerate 7 or 8 minutes. Some communities want 50 percent of each shift to be spent on proactive patrol; some are willing to get by on 15 percent. Some communities want extensive traffic enforcement; some do not. Some communities want high patrol visibility in residential neighborhoods; for others, one drive through a neighborhood every 2 weeks is plenty. There is no "rule" requiring that at least one patrol officer always be available in a jurisdiction for a true 911 emergency, but most jurisdictions want there to be at least one unit free all, or nearly all, of the time. Other communities enjoy readily available back-up units for true emergencies, such as contiguous jurisdictions or a university campus police department within the jurisdiction, and can therefore staff at lower levels. Addressing the above issues, in reality, provides the answer to the question "How many patrol officers are needed?" And once this question is answered, the officers assigned to patrol are required to be multitaskers. They are concurrently responding to service demand, both critical and noncritical, maintaining spatial and time distribution to assure rapid response to emergency situations, providing reassuring visibility to a community, engaging in active crime deterrent efforts, and remaining alert on emergency standby for truly critical situations.

Many police agencies continue to cling to allocation models that are both out-dated and insufficient to meet the array of demands identified above. In fact, some departments still allocate by geography, assigning 1 officer per beat 24 hours a day, 7 days a week, without regards to calls for service or crime patterns while others focus on police/population ratios, which are not at all reflective of the level of police service provided to a community. In many police departments, the process of making patrol allocation decisions has been a haphazard process that has been influenced by both political and financial considerations completely apart from considerations of how many people it takes to do the work the police are expected to do in the way they are expected to do it.

Over time, allocation models have become more sophisticated and have taken into account more and more factors in determining allocation needs. For example, the latest generation of allocation models, which were discussed in chapter 3, such as the Model for the Allocation of Patrol Personnel (MAPP), takes several factors into account in determining the number of officers that need to be assigned to patrol. This chapter provides a discussion of several factors that impact police patrol allocation. Police administrators need to take these variables or factors into account when determining how many officers need to be assigned to the patrol function. Furthermore, how policy decisions affect patrol allocation will be illustrated.

FACTORS THAT IMPACT ALLOCATION OF POLICE PATROL

Factors that impact allocation of police patrol can be divided based on their source. First, some of the factors that impact allocation are data-driven and therefore are derived from department records or other city departments. Variables such as the number of calls for service and number of roadway miles in a jurisdiction fit into this category. Second, some of the factors that impact allocation are best categorized as policy decisions made by police administrators. Variables such as response time goals and visibility objectives fit into this category. The following sections will discuss the variables that impact allocation of police patrol and thus the number of officers that need to be assigned to this function.

Data-Driven Variables

As mentioned above, some variables that impact allocation are data-driven and when used in an allocation model are obtained from department records or other government agencies. Each of these variables will be discussed below.

Calls for Service

Obviously, the number of calls for service a department receives impacts the allocation of officers to patrol. Agencies with more calls for service need to assign more officers to patrol in comparison to agencies with fewer calls for service. When used in an allocation model, the value for this variable should include all calls for service for a particular time frame. Typically, allocation models are based on 1 year of call for service data. However, these models can frequently be used to determine fluctuations in the need for officers assigned to patrol based on seasonal variations in calls for service. Therefore, the number of calls for service for each month could be identified, and these numbers are used to understand fluctuations in the number of personnel that need to be assigned to patrol by month. This can assist an administrator in determining when the best months are to have substantial training provided to officers, when vacation time should be taken, and when officers should be encouraged to take compensatory time. The numbers of calls for service should also take into account back-up units as well. Administrative and self-initiated activities are typically excluded from calls-for-service numbers in allocation models since these activities are taken into account through policy decisions that will be discussed in a later section of this chapter.

Therefore, calls-for-service workload is a key factor in determining the number of patrol officers needed. The choices that police administrators make on how to handle this workload has an important impact on the number of patrol officers required to serve a community. Some would argue that the management of calls-for-service workload is largely beyond the control of police administrators, but the reality is that police can, in collaboration with political and community leaders, devise viable strategies for handling these demands. Some police departments, for example, have stopped investigating non-injury auto accidents while others continue to engage in this practice. Some have stopped responding to unverified alarm calls at businesses and residences. It is common for alarm calls to account for 10–20 percent of the calls for service a department receives. Nationally about 98 percent of the alarm calls the police respond to are false, and they have a significant effect on police workload and staffing levels. There are a number of cities that have adopted a "verified" response policy, which essentially is a policy that says the police will not respond to an alarm call unless it has been verified that a crime has actually occurred. Furthermore, some departments use non-sworn officers or volunteers to handle certain types of calls.

The ability of a police department to engage in community policing, problem solving, or any type of police service for that matter is heavily influenced by call management practices and policies. The police have an enormous number of choices on how to respond to the various expectations of the community. Should police officers respond to all calls for service? Can non-sworn personnel handle some of the calls? Can some reports or calls be handled over the telephone? Should police investigate non-injury traffic accidents? What opportunities does technology and the Internet present for managing police calls? Many departments have placed significant emphasis on managing calls for service and seeking alternative methods in order to maximize the time officers have on the street for other responsibilities. The end result of these call management practices is fewer calls for service that require an officer to respond. Thus, fewer calls for service equates to fewer patrol officers required for this specific patrol task.

Service Time

Average service time is another variable that impacts patrol allocation. It is calculated based on the elapsed time from when an officer is dispatched to when an officer clears the call. Average service time is usually calculated based on the total number of calls for service, not on specific types of calls for service. This value represents the average amount of time taken to handle a call for service. If back-up units are not accounted for in the calculation of the total number of calls for service, then they need to be taken into consideration when calculating average service time. Basically, an administrator is attempting to account for all the time the officers spend on calls for service, including back-up units. For example, if one call for service takes 45 minutes but two back-up units respond, the call did not take 45 minutes of personnel time. Instead, this one call actually took 2 hours and 15 minutes of personnel time to complete (45 minutes (X) 3 officers = 2 hours and 15 minutes). If back-up units are not taken into consideration when determining the number of officers that need to be assigned to patrol, staffing levels in patrol will be too low. Therefore, back-up units need to be taken into consideration either in determining the total number of calls for service or in calculating average service time.

Roadway Miles (Impacts Visibility)

Patrol visibility is a concern for citizens and police administrators alike. The public wants the police to be visible in their communities and in their neighborhoods. The level of visibility of officers obviously impacts the number of officers that need to be assigned to patrol. Agencies with a commitment to high visibility in their community will need more officers assigned to patrol than agencies with less commitment. In order to accomplish visibility goals, allocation models need to take into account the number of roadway miles within a given jurisdiction to determine the number of officers needed to satisfy the subjective demands of citizens and police administrators. As will be discussed in a later section of this chapter, visibility standards are typically set for two types of roadways: major and residential. Major roadways include freeways, highways, and other major thoroughfares. The police department may not have this information within its records, but the number of roadway miles broken down by type of roadway can typically be obtained from another government agency such as the Department of Transportation or the Public Works Department. Obviously, the number of roadway miles impacts the number of patrol officers needed. Agencies with fewer roadway miles will need fewer officers to accomplish the visibility objective for patrol.

Patrol Speed (Impacts Visibility)

Similarly, the speed at which officers drive on major and residential roadways impacts the department's level of visibility and thus patrol staffing needs. Therefore, in order to determine the number of officers needed to meet the visibility standards set by agency administration, the average patrol speed on major and residential roadways is also needed. Basically, the previous two variables impact allocation because how visible officers can be varies by the number of roadway miles in a jurisdiction and how fast officers typically travel on these roadways. Fewer officers are obviously needed for visibility purposes when an agency has 100 miles of roadway in which officers typically travel 30 mph in comparison to another agency that is responsible for over 500 miles of roadway in which officers typically travel 25 mph.

Although the technology exists to determine average patrol speed by roadway type, most agencies do not have these data. If an agency does not have these data, one alternative is to use the average patrol speed from comparable cities that have these data. Another alternative is to use patrol speeds determined from prior patrol allocation studies. Although these alternatives are not ideal because they introduce error into an allocation model, it may be the only practical alternative for some agencies.

As an example, the average patrol speed on major roadways in prior allocation studies conducted by the authors is 24.5 mph. Similarly, the average patrol speed on residential roadways in prior allocation studies is 13.5 mph. These values may seem to be low, but they take into account the time not only when a patrol vehicle is moving but also when it is at stop lights/signs, in traffic, as well as other circumstances when the vehicle may not be moving at all or only moving at a low rate of speed.

Geographic Area (Impacts Response Time)
The area, in square miles, of a jurisdiction is taken into account in allocation models when determining the number of officers needed to meet the response time goals set by the police department. For example, the formula presented in chapter 3 is used in several allocation models to determine the average number of on-duty officers required per day to meet a response time objective for nonemergency activities.

Response Speed (Impacts Response Time)
In addition to the area, in square miles, the average response speed for emergency and non-emergency calls for service is taken into account in allocation models in determining the number of officers needed to meet the response time goals set by the police department. Like the issue associated with determining average patrol speed, values for the response speed for emergency and non-emergency calls are commonly not available to many agencies. If this is the case, then this value can be derived from prior allocation studies and/or other comparable jurisdictions.

Leave Rate
The leave rate also has a significant impact on allocation decisions. This rate is calculated by collecting and analyzing key "time off" data. An accurate leave rate is crucial to the accuracy of patrol allocation decisions and the determination of the number of officers that need to be assigned to patrol. The leave rate for an agency is frequently underestimated, and it is argued that high overtime costs, the inability to cover some beats, the

inability to free officers for training, and other staffing level issues can be attributed to inaccurately calculating the actual number of hours officers are available to work on patrol each year.

Typically, each officer is contracted to work 2,086 hours per year (40 hours per week ($\times$) 52.14 weeks per year). However, an officer does not actually work the entire 2,086 hours. There are numerous instances in which officers may not actually be available to patrol during the 2,086 hours they are contracted to work. In order to accurately determine the net annual work hours per officer, all instances in which an officer is not available to work on patrol must be taken into consideration; these include the following:

- Vacation time
- Use of compensatory time
- Sick leave
- Training
- Holidays
- Personal days
- Military service
- Provisions of the Family and Medical Leave Act
- Light-duty assignments required for injured staff
- Time away from patrol while on special assignments
- Jury duty
- Worker's compensation time off
- Administrative leave.

By taking the above factors into account, it may be determined that out of the 2,086 hours officers are contracted to work each year, they are available to work on patrol for only 1,550 hours each year. It is crucial that the net annual work hours are calculated accurately, because if it is inaccurate it can have a significant impact on staffing and coverage levels. The net annual work hours can then be used to calculate the leave rate by subtracting the net annual work hours from the number of hours officers are contracted to work each year. The result of this subtraction is then divided by the number of hours officers are contracted to work each year to obtain the leave rate.

A corollary to the leave rate is the "relief factor." Since patrol officers must be on the street 24 hours a day, 365 days a year, the "relief factor" is used to determine how many officers are required to fill one position around the clock 365 days a year. For a 5-day, 8-hour-per-day work week with typical benefits, it requires almost six patrol officers to staff one patrol position around the clock 365 days a year.

Policy Variables

Policy decisions have a significant impact on allocation of patrol personnel as well. Several factors that impact allocation can be considered policy decisions. Police administrators set values for these variables, and they can be modified by the department as the policies change. For example, if an administrator believes that the response time goal for emergency calls for service is too high, another lower value can be set and the number of officers needed to meet this new objective can be determined by an allocation model. There is no right or wrong value for any of the policy decisions that impact allocation. It is based on the level of service that a police department wants to provide to its citizens and based on the availability of resources needed to meet the performance objectives set for patrol. Each of the policy decisions that impacts allocation of police patrol is discussed below.

Policing Service Model

The approach a department takes to policing has a significant impact on the staffing levels required. If a department chooses not to engage in community or problem-oriented policing then time does not have to be set aside for these activities. If a department uses a split-force concept in which one group of officers responds to calls for service and another has the community policing responsibilities, it will affect the number of officers required for each function. Similarly, as previously discussed, the call management practices and policies established by administrators have a significant impact on the allocation of patrol resources. For example, if an administrator believes that an officer should respond, in person, to every citizen's request for police service, then more officers will be needed in comparison to more restrictive service models.

Visibility Objective

A visibility objective is used in some allocation models to determine the number of officers needed for patrol visibility. The visibility objective is based on the answer to this question, how often should a patrol officer pass any given point on a roadway? Basically, if a person was to stand on a roadway, how often should he or she see a patrol officer? Typically, two visibility objectives are established based on the two types of roadways previously mentioned: major and residential roadways. It is expected that officers will be more visible on major roadways in comparison to residential roadways; therefore a separate visibility objective is set for each type of roadway in some allocation models.

The visibility objective is a policy decision that must be made by police administrators to fit the needs of their community. For example, in test cities that implemented the Patrol Allocation Model (PAM), which was discussed in chapter 3, the average visibility objective was 2.33 hours for major roadways. Therefore, it is expected that an officer will pass a given point on a major roadway every 2.33 hours. This value, however, may be too high or low for many police administrators. Some administrators may be satisfied with a visibility objective of several hours while others may want a 1-hour visibility objective on major roadways. These policy decisions allow administrators an opportunity to set standards for the level of police service they want to provide to the community.

It is also important to note that the visibility objective is basically an average. Therefore, there will be some major roadways in which an officer is seen more frequently than the set visibility objective. Likewise, there will be some major roadways in which an officer is seen less frequently than the set objective.

A separate visibility objective for residential roadways is also established by police administrators. As residential visibility becomes a concern for citizens and administrators, the visibility objective can be lowered and the number of officers that need to be assigned to patrol to meet this new performance objective can be determined. Administrators decide the values for these variables and thus the level of visibility of patrol in the community. Obviously, higher levels of patrol visibility will require that more officers be assigned to patrol. Likewise, lower levels of patrol visibility will require fewer officers.

Response Time

Response time is a central component in patrol resource allocation. If the department establishes an inappropriate response time goal, it will have an enormous effect on the number of police officers required to meet the goal. In the 1972 report of the National Advisory Commission on Criminal Justice Standards and Goals, the response time standard was set at three to 5 minutes for all part one crime calls. This was an impossible standard to meet and one that made little sense when it was understood that most of these calls were not emergencies and 67 percent of these crimes were discovered sometime after they had occurred. Therefore, departments establish response time goals that distinguish between emergency and non-emergency calls for service using a priority system.

The response time goals are set by police administrators and used in allocation models to determine the number of officers needed to meet the response time objectives. If response time goals are set fairly high, then fewer officers will need to be assigned to patrol to meet this objective in comparison to when response time goals are set fairly low. As with all the policy decisions, these values can be modified as changes in policy occur. In other words, a department may have a 6-minute response time goal for emergency calls, and patrol is staffed at a level to meet this goal. If the administration decides to lower this goal to 5 minutes, allocation models can be used to determine the number of officers to meet the new response time goal of 5 minutes to emergency calls.

Officer Availability to Respond to Emergencies

It is necessary for agencies to have officers available on patrol who can immediately respond to an emergency. The percentage of time that an agency wants at least one officer available to immediately respond to an emergency call for service impacts allocation. An agency will need more officers if administrators want an officer immediately available 95 percent of the time in comparison to an agency that wants officers immediately available 75 percent of the time. Since emergency calls are potentially life-threatening, the percentage set for this objective is typically very high.

When allocation models determine the number of officers for this purpose, it is assumed that there are occasions when an officer who is on another call for service can clear that call and respond to the emergency call. When the officer is finished responding to the emergency call, then the officer can return to the previous call if another officer has not already covered it. Therefore, a certain percentage of calls for service can be preempted if an officer is needed to respond to an emergency call for service. However, it is also argued that some calls for service cannot or should not be preempted because of the severity of the call for service or because of dissatisfaction among citizens. Therefore, the percentage of calls for service that cannot be preempted is a policy decision, and its value impacts patrol allocation. The same is true for administrative activities and self-initiated patrol activities; some of these activities can be preempted so an officer can respond to an emergency call. The percentage of time calls can and cannot be preempted is a policy decision that must be made by police administrators.

Administrative Activities

Time spent on administrative activities significantly impacts police patrol allocation. Allocation models take into account the administrative time an officer spends on duty in determining the number of officers needed for patrol allocation. Administrative time can include meal breaks, other breaks, vehicle maintenance, roll call, court time, as well as other administrative activities. Administrative time can be set similar to a performance objective. In other words, how many minutes should an officer spend on administrative activities? This is a policy decision, which can certainly be influenced by data. For example, data can be collected on the amount of time officers spend in court, eating meals and taking other breaks (per shift), and attending to vehicle maintenance (e.g., putting gas in the patrol vehicle). The data can be used by administrators in determining the appropriate value that should be set for the administrative time allotted per officer. Obviously, the higher the value set for this variable, the more officers that will need to be assigned to patrol.

Self-Initiated Activity

The amount of time officers spend on self-initiated activities also impacts allocation decisions. Agencies that expect patrol officers to conduct numerous traffic stops, stop suspicious individuals, target "hot spots," and perform other self-initiated activities during their shift will require more officers assigned to patrol in comparison to agencies that do not emphasize self-initiated activities as much. In addition, a portion of self-initiated officer activity is not discretionary such as the occurrence of an accident or fight in front of an officer. The time officers spend on self-initiated activities is taken into account in some allocation models. The self-initiated time can also be set similar to a performance objective. This policy decision is based on the answer to the question, how many minutes per hour should an officer spend on self-initiated activities? Unlike the administrative activity discussed above, it is generally not recommended that data on self-initiated activities largely influence this policy decision. Assessing prior practice does not necessarily mean that an adequate amount of time for self-initiated activities was afforded to officers. Administrators may want more self-initiated activities performed than current practice dictates.

Unrecoverable Patrol Time

Several allocation models try to account for all the time officers spend on calls for service, administrative activities, self-initiated activities as well as efforts to meet performance objectives such as visibility and response time. It is recognized that some patrol time is not used for any of the above purposes and thus can be classified as unrecoverable. In other words, the time period is too short to increase visibility, to perform a self-initiated activity, or to conduct an administrative activity. This includes short periods of time between the clearing of one call and the receiving of another. For example, it is common for an officer to clear a call and receive another within a few minutes. In this example, there is not enough time between calls for the officer to accomplish other tasks. This also includes time when an officer is stuck in traffic and other occasions as well. This time can be considered unrecoverable patrol time because it cannot be used to meet the performance objectives established by the department.

There is yet another way to conceptualize unrecoverable patrol time. Handling police calls for service is inherently stressful. The police overwhelmingly deal with conflict management. Repeatedly jumping from one conflict situation to another takes a psychological toll on officers. It may simply not be realistic to have an expectation that officers can do this night after night, week after week, month after month, without a break. The unrecoverable patrol time might also be regarded as recovery time for officers. They need some time to calm down, regroup, think through what just occurred, and prepare psychologically for the next conflict that will have to be refereed.

There are professions, albeit very few, in which practitioners do indeed move steadily from one stressful situation to another. Emergency medical technicians in very busy districts is one example, emergency room physicians another. But there is an element in policing that these professionals do not need to deal with-the ever-present threat of personal assault. Policing is inherently far more dangerous than statistics indicate. The only reason we do not have a far greater number of officers injured or killed than we do is because we train and retrain to use strong precaution. Therefore, unrecoverable patrol time can also be considered recovery time.

Two-Officer Patrol Units

Decisions on patrol allocation need to take into consideration and make adjustments for the percentage of time patrol units are staffed with two officers. Two-officer units do reduce the need for back-up units to certain calls for service, but two-officer units are not twice as capable as one-officer units of meeting the stated performance objectives for patrol. For example, a two-officer unit is not twice as visible as a one-officer unit. Likewise, a two-officer unit cannot respond twice as fast to a call for service as a one-officer unit. Therefore, the percentage of time patrol units are staffed with two officers has an impact on police patrol allocation. The value set for this variable in allocation models is a policy decision because the department can set the percentage of time that is acceptable to have two-officer units. It is important to note that even in agencies that deploy 100 percent one-officer units, there will often be two-officer units deployed for field training of recruits and deployed during the period when there is an increase in vehicle maintenance problems and this must be taken into consideration when making allocation decisions.

HOW POLICY DECISIONS AFFECT PATROL ALLOCATION

This section is designed to discuss how the policy decisions discussed above, and changes in policy decisions, affect the number of officers that need to be assigned to patrol. Administrators set values for these variables for use in allocation models, and they can be modified by the department as the policies change. For example, if it is believed that a value is too high or low, then another value can be set and the number of officers needed to meet this new objective can be determined. Therefore, each time a policy decision is changed, a different number of officers needs to be assigned to patrol. Changes in some policy decisions can have a significant impact on allocation needs.

The following examples use the MAPP, discussed in chapter 3, to calculate the number of officers that need to be assigned to patrol. A few examples will be provided in order to demonstrate the impact that modifications of policy decisions have on the number of officers which need to be assigned to patrol. For each of the examples below, the values set for each policy decision are provided in a table. Example 1 will serve as the base. In other words, it is assumed that taking into account all of the data-driven and policy variables utilized in the MAPP, 577 officers need to be assigned to patrol. The values for the data-driven variables are not presented in the tables; only the values for the policy variables are given. The values for the data-driven variables remain constant in each example; only the values for one or more policy variables have changed.

Example 1

Example 1 is based on the following values:

Policy Decisions	
1) Visibility objective (hours), major roadways	3.5
2) Visibility objective (hours), residential roadways	36
3) Response time objective for emergency calls (minutes)	6.5
4) Response time objective for non-emergency calls (minutes)	15
5) Percentage of emergency calls for which there will be at least one officer available	98
6) Percentage of calls for service that cannot be preempted	60
7) Percentage of administrative activities that cannot be preempted	25
8) Percentage of self-initiated activities that cannot be preempted	60
9) Administrative time in minutes per hour per officer	10
10) Self-initiated time in minutes per hour per officer	10
11) Unrecoverable patrol time in minutes per hour per officer	5
12) Percentage of time patrol units are staffed with two officers	10

When these values are used in the MAPP model along with values for the data-driven variables, it is estimated that **577** officers need to be assigned to patrol. The assignment of 577 officers to patrol would allow the department to meet the performance objectives established involving response time, visibility, and availability to respond to emergency calls. In addition, officers would have about 10 minutes per hour (about 17 percent of shift) for administrative activities and 10 minutes per hour (about 17 percent of shift) for self-initiated activities.

Example 2

In Example 2, the values for the data-driven variables used in Example 1 remain the same, only one of the policy decisions has changed (percentage of time patrol units are staffed with two officers). Example 2 is based on the following values:

Policy Decisions	
1) Visibility objective (hours), major roadways	3.5
2) Visibility objective (hours), residential roadways	36
3) Response time objective for emergency calls (minutes)	6.5
4) Response time objective for non-emergency calls (minutes)	15
5) Percentage of emergency calls for which there will be at least one officer available	98

6) Percentage of calls for service that cannot be preempted	60
7) Percentage of administrative activities that cannot be preempted	25
8) Percentage of self-initiated activities that cannot be preempted	60
9) Administrative time in minutes per hour per officer	10
10) Self-initiated time in minutes per hour per officer	10
11) Unrecoverable patrol time in minutes per hour per officer	5
12) Percentage of time patrol units are staffed with two officers	0

When this modification is made, it is estimated that **523** officers need to be assigned to patrol, a difference of 54 fewer officers in comparison to Example 1. It is important to note that the department will still be able to meet the performance objectives set in the first example as well as have the same amount of time for administrative and self-initiated activities. Example 2 illustrates the isolated cost of two-officer units.

Example 3

Example 3 is based on the following values (once again the values for the data-driven variables remain the same):

Policy Decisions	
1) Visibility objective (hours), major roadways	3.5
2) Visibility objective (hours), residential roadways	49.6
3) Response time objective for emergency calls (minutes)	6.5
4) Response time objective for non-emergency calls (minutes)	15
5) Percentage of emergency calls for which there will be at least one officer available	98
6) Percentage of calls for service that cannot be preempted	60
7) Percentage of administrative activities that cannot be preempted	25
8) Percentage of self-initiated activities that cannot be preempted	60
9) Administrative time in minutes per hour per officer	10
10) Self-initiated time in minutes per hour per officer	10
11) Unrecoverable patrol time in minutes per hour per officer	5
12) Percentage of time patrol units are staffed with two officers	2

Two modifications are made in this example in comparison to the first example. First, the percentage of time patrol units are staffed with two officers is set at 2 percent instead of 10 percent. It allows for a few instances in which two officer units should be deployed. In addition, the visibility objective on residential roadways is set at 49.6 hours instead of 36 hours. The value of 49.6 hours is the average for the test cities throughout the country that implemented the PAM. When these modifications are made, it is estimated that **524** officers need to be assigned to patrol, a difference of 53 fewer officers in comparison to the first example but only one more officer in comparison to Example 2. It allows for the ability to use two-officer units occasionally as well as increases the visibility objective on residential roadways. Therefore, officers will be somewhat less visible on residential roadways in comparison to the first example, but the department will still be able to meet the other performance objectives as well as allocate time for administrative and self-initiated activities.

Example 4

Example 4 is based on the following values (once again the values for the data-driven variables remain the same):

Policy Decisions	
1) Visibility objective (hours), major roadways	3.5
2) Visibility objective (hours), residential roadways	36
3) Response time objective for emergency calls (minutes)	6.5
4) Response time objective for non-emergency calls (minutes)	15
5) Percentage of emergency calls for which there will be at least one officer available	98
6) Percentage of calls for service that cannot be preempted	60
7) Percentage of administrative activities that cannot be preempted	25
8) Percentage of self-initiated activities that cannot be preempted	60
9) Administrative time in minutes per hour per officer	10
10) Self-initiated time in minutes per hour per officer	20
11) Unrecoverable patrol time in minutes per hour per officer	2.5
12) Percentage of time patrol units are staffed with two officers	10

Two modifications are made in this example in comparison to the first example. First, the amount of time for self-initiated activities is doubled, from 10 minutes (about 17 percent of shift) to 20 minutes (33 percent of shift) per hour. It can be argued that 10 minutes per hour for these activities is not enough to allow an officer to effectively perform self-initiated activities. Second, the amount of unrecoverable patrol time is reduced to half, from 5 to 2.5 minutes per hour per officer. Allowing for 5 minutes per hour per officer for unrecoverable patrol time may be seen as too much by some police administrators. Making these modifications has a significant effect on the number of officers that need to be assigned to patrol. It is estimated that **728** officers need to be assigned to patrol to meet the performance objectives set in this example. This is an increase of 151 officers in comparison to the first example which equates to a 26 percent increase in patrol officers.

DISCUSSION

As demonstrated in this chapter, the answer to the question, "How many patrol officers?" varies based on several factors. Although comparable police citizen ratios are slightly relevant, they do not provide a definitive answer to the question. A better approach is the use of a performance-based allocation tool, such as the Model for the Allocation of Patrol Personnel, described in chapter 3. Even then, however, questions are left unanswered. The MAPP model calls for the user to specify several "performance variables." These include the amount of time officers spend on proactive efforts. Proactive efforts include activities ranging from traffic law enforcement to attending community meetings. These are policy decisions for which there is no "outside answer." It depends upon what a given community wants to "purchase" in policing services.

The question then becomes, which of the above examples is right? The answer is that which is right is the wrong question. Each example estimates the number of officers that need to be assigned to patrol to meet the performance objectives set by the policy decisions. These examples demonstrate the critical importance of making logical and well thought out policy decisions on these variables. Saying that officers should be visible on a residential street every 5 hours has significant ramifications on the number of officers that needs to be assigned to patrol. Similarly, using two-officer units, allocating a significant amount of time for self-initiated activities, and making any other modifications to the values used in allocation models can have a significant impact on the bottom line: the number of officers that needs to be assigned to patrol. There should be consensus among the command staff of a department regarding which values should be set for these policy decisions and then patrol should be staffed based on the results of the allocation model utilized by the department. Staffing patrol to the level recommended by an allocation model will allow a department to meet the performance objectives set by the policy decisions. If patrol is not staffed to those requirements, then the performance objectives will not be met.

Patrol Deployment

CHAPTER

$$\boxed{5}$$

Deployment Through Scheduling

INTRODUCTION

Once the variables that impact allocation have been explored by an agency and a determination of the number of patrol officers needed to provide service to the community has been made, the deployment of these officers is addressed. The need to respond to service requests 24 hours a day, 7 days a week requires that some level of patrol presence be deployed at all times. To provide such availability and coverage, administrators have experimented with a variety of scheduling plans and procedures. Some plans have been met with a great deal of success while others have failed quickly. The variation in scheduling practices among departments is based on numerous factors including management objectives, administrative issues, local traditions, and the absence of scheduling information.[1] The objectives to be met by a schedule play a major role in determining its particular features and characteristics. For example, a schedule that maximizes the number of weekends off for patrol officers may not match the administration's objectives of providing increased patrol coverage on Friday and Saturday evenings when call loads are highest. In addition to management objectives, the types of work schedules that can be used are limited by the administrative rules and procedures of a particular agency. For example, if city policy mandates that all city employees work exactly 80 hours during each biweekly paycheck period, this will eliminate some scheduling plans as options for a particular agency.[2]

Furthermore, the variety of police scheduling plans is also influenced by local traditions. The influence of tradition within an agency cannot be minimized because it impacts scheduling practices in many agencies. The attitude of "that is the way it has always been done around here" inhibits some administrators from carefully analyzing potential changes to work schedules that will benefit the department and the community. Lastly, the variety of police scheduling methods in each agency is partly due to the lack of scheduling information available to administrators. The analysis, design, and implementation of police work schedules has not been routinely included as topics within training courses for administrators nor are these topics routinely included in supervision and administration textbooks in the field. Furthermore, the description of schedules in most police journals and reports are based on one individual agency. In other words, they are frequently the descriptions of what a particular agency is doing which makes it difficult to evaluate whether certain core features of the schedule may be applicable to other agencies. This has resulted in an environment where administrators responsible for scheduling do not have significant resources to draw upon in developing effective schedules for their agencies.[3]

Scheduling is a method police administrators can use to improve the operational efficiency of their agency. If the current work schedule is ineffective, then a new schedule can make more personnel available when they are needed. No patrol shift schedule will work for every police department. A patrol schedule should be based on the needs of the agency and the community. Patrol officers should be deployed where they are needed, when they are needed, and in proportion to the workload (i.e., calls for service). Therefore, the objective of this chapter is not to lobby for a particular type of scheduling for patrol. Instead, this chapter will review the benefits of an effective scheduling plan. Three main types of scheduling plans will be discussed as well as the benefits and drawbacks of each plan. Along with these three scheduling plans, various scheduling alternatives including overlapping shifts, power shifts, and variable shift start times will be reviewed. Furthermore, various scheduling issues will be analyzed including shift rotation, days off rotation, proportional scheduling, scheduling vacation, and other issues.

BENEFITS OF AN EFFECTIVE SCHEDULING PLAN

There are several benefits of an effective scheduling plan that will be presented in this section. It is important to note that not all of the benefits can be obtained through the use of one particular scheduling plan. The scheduling plans discussed in a later section of this chapter can assist an agency in maximizing some of the benefits of an effective scheduling plan. However, there is no ideal scheduling plan that will allow an agency to attain all of the benefits noted in this section. In fact, when certain benefits are maximized in a particular scheduling plan, other benefits are more difficult to attain. For example, the overlapping of shifts available in some scheduling plans allows for increased communication between officers assigned to various shifts. However, more efficient use of equipment, including vehicles and radios, is typically accomplished by not overlapping shifts. In overlapping shifts, more vehicles and radios and other equipment are needed because more officers are on-duty at one time than occurs in scheduling plans that do not overlap shifts.

There are several noted benefits of an effective scheduling plan. First, an effective scheduling plan maximizes officers' availability to cover workload demands. This benefit is central to the patrol function. The primary police mission is to provide service to the community 24 hours a day, 7 days a week. However, demand for police service varies between communities and varies by time of day and day of week. Within a particular agency, calls for service typically follow a predictable pattern by day of week and time of day. Therefore, an effective schedule takes this pattern into account in deploying officers on the street available for service at the right times and in the right places.[4] An effective schedule will provide the appropriate number of officers needed for each day of the week and each shift.

Second, an effective schedule can lead to a reduction in fatigue among officers. Fatigue is a "mental and/or physical state resulting from insufficient good-quality sleep or from prolonged or intense physical, emotional, or mental effort that tends to decrease alertness, impair performance potential, worsen mood, and interfere with decision making."[5] Fatigue is not good in any profession, but it is particularly problematic in law enforcement considering the potential consequences of decreased alertness while on-duty, impaired performance, and poor decision-making. In fact, studies have shown that after about 18 hours of staying awake, a person's performance is impaired to the same level as someone who has 0.05 percent blood alcohol content.[6] Staying awake for 24 hours can produce impairment similar to 0.10 percent blood alcohol content, which is above the legal intoxication level in all states.[7]

It is obviously not practical for a police administrator to say that in the interest of reducing fatigue, officers will no longer be assigned to the night shift because it interferes with their circadian rhythms (a person's sleep/wake cycle). However, it is important for administrators to understand the primary sources of fatigue and to try to reduce fatigue through effective scheduling practices. The most common sources of fatigue that an administrator may have control over is poor shift rotation schemes, excessive overtime assignments, frequent off-duty court appearances, the use of double shifts in order to deal with personnel shortages, and frequent off-duty security positions.[8] Other sources of officer fatigue cannot be controlled by an administrator, especially those that derive from the personal lives of officers, but it is important for administrators to minimize the sources of fatigue within their control.

Third, an effective schedule can increase communication between officers assigned to various shifts. Administrators frequently report that inadequate information is exchanged between officers assigned to different shifts. The officers coming off-duty have just completed their shift, are tired, and want to be on their way. Information about suspects, locations to be watched, and developing situations may not be passed along to the officers coming on-duty. In agencies that see this as a significant problem, scheduling adjustments can be made to provide for greater opportunity for information exchange. Overlapping shifts by several minutes is one practice that is helpful in obtaining this benefit. Officers can be scheduled so that shifts overlap, typically for up to 60 minutes, to provide for both continuous service and an opportunity for information exchange at shift changes.[9]

Fourth, an effective scheduling plan can maximize the quality of family/leisure time. It is easy to say that work and family shall not mix. The reality is that each one has a significant impact on the other. Excessive work demands caused by poor scheduling can lead to significant family problems for an officer. A schedule that requires an officer to work the evening shift, with no rotation with fixed weekdays off, may restrict an officer's ability to spend time with his/her family and thus cause significant family problems for the officer. It is obviously impossible to have all officers work the day shift with weekends off, but an effective schedule provides the benefit of enhancing quality family and leisure time for an officer as much as possible.

Fifth, an effective schedule can lead to a reduction in sick leave taken by officers. Sick leave is obviously designed to be used when officers are actually sick. However, sick leave is frequently used by officers to get a day off in the middle of their work week or to extend the number of days off at the end of the work week. Many departments periodically analyze the amount of sick leave taken by hour of day, day of week, day in the schedule cycle, shift, length of leave taken, circumstances of return, etc.[10] An effective schedule is one that does not encourage unnecessary sick leave.

Sixth, another benefit of an effective scheduling plan is high officer morale. High morale is reflected in job satisfaction and organizational commitment and loyalty. This can lead to greater quality of work, less absenteeism due to sickness, lower turnover rates, and more.[11] It has been argued that improving a work schedule can have as much impact on officer satisfaction as an increase in pay.[12] Officers do not want to work schedules that interfere with their ability to perform their duties in a safe and effective manner. Therefore, schedules that involve long hours, long intervals without time off, or frequent shift changes cause significant stress and fatigue for officers.[13] A schedule that minimizes these effects will lead to higher satisfaction and morale among officers.

Seventh, a police agency may also be able to save money and resources by implementing an effective scheduling plan. For example, it is seen as ineffective to schedule officers equally among shifts because calls for service and other workload measures do not occur equally over the course of a day. Therefore, an effective scheduling plan can make the necessary modifications to the work schedule by having the correct number of officers available at the right time. This benefit is similar to the one discussed above that noted an effective scheduling plan maximizes officer's availability to cover workload demands. An agency may discover that through the use of overlapping or power shifts they can provide the same level of service to citizens with actually fewer officers. It is important to understand that effective scheduling does not guarantee to save money or resources. In fact, some scheduling plans that are discussed in this chapter actually require more resources to implement.

Eighth, an effective scheduling plan can lead to a reduction in overtime expenditures. This has been alluded to earlier but should be considered as a separate potential benefit of effective scheduling practices. For example, if officers are assigned in equal numbers to various shifts, overtime expenditures frequently increase on the shifts with greater workload. Through the use of proportional scheduling (i.e., assigning officers to shifts based on workload demands), overtime expenditures may be reduced. Furthermore, effective scheduling of vacations, compensatory time, and other time off for officers can also lead to a reduction in overtime expenditures. Also, the use of overlapping shifts may reduce overtime use because officers coming off-duty will have time to finish paperwork and take care of other responsibilities while the officers coming on-duty cover calls for service.

Lastly, another benefit of effective scheduling practices is more efficient use of equipment. Scheduling is typically thought of as only impacting the need for officers and determining the number of officers that need to be assigned to each shift, each day of the week. However, these officers obviously need the necessary equipment (vehicles, radios, etc.) to effectively perform their duties. Scheduling practices can lead to more efficient use of equipment. For example, in schedules that do not overlap, officers coming off-duty typically give their equipment to the officers coming on duty for use on the next shift. This type of schedule (non-overlapping) typically requires less equipment than overlapping schedules. Overlapping schedules typically require more equipment because more officers are on the street at one time.

Another way to look at the benefits of an effective scheduling plan is that it attempts to overcome the following scheduling issues:

- Matching staff level to the demand for service;
- Revising schedules to accommodate vacations, sick-time, compensatory time, leaves, and other personnel matters;
- Designing the schedule to satisfy legal constraints, governmental policy directives, or collective bargaining agreements;
- Equipment shortages during periods of peak staffing;
- Inadequate times between shifts at changeover times;
- Fairness in the scheduling of holidays and weekend days;
- Lack of communication between personnel assigned to the various shifts;
- Accommodating training, meetings, special assignments, and other administrative demands into the work schedule;
- Restrictions on outside activities such as education and extra employment due to variability in the work schedule (including shift changes); and
- Employee fatigue, boredom, and/or low morale associated with scheduling problems.[14]

No scheduling plan will be able to overcome all of these scheduling problems, but attempts can be made to maximize the attainable benefits of an effective scheduling plan.

SCHEDULING PLANS

At their most basic, scheduling plans typically vary on the number of days worked per week and number of hours worked per shift. Other issues are also addressed by scheduling plans including whether the shifts are rotating or fixed, whether days off rotate or not, how many shifts will be used, at what time shifts will begin, and the degree of overlap between shifts. These issues will be discussed in a later section of this chapter. In this section, the three most common scheduling plans (5-8, 4-10, and 3-12) will be discussed. It is important to understand that there are several variations of these plans actually in use in law enforcement agencies throughout the country. However, the idiosyncrasies of the numerous variations of these scheduling plans are beyond the scope of this chapter. The basic scheduling plans will be discussed along with their benefits and drawbacks, which are based on information derived from agencies that have implemented the various plans and from literature in the field. The benefits and drawbacks of each plan are not guaranteed to occur in each jurisdiction that utilizes one of these scheduling plans. They are benefits and drawbacks experienced by agencies in the past and may not completely apply to a particular agency.

5-8 Scheduling

Under a 5-8 scheduling plan, an officer works five 8-hour shifts and gets two days off. This scheduling plan is also frequently referred to as a 5-2 schedule with 5 representing the number of consecutive days worked and 2 representing the number of consecutive days off. In this chapter, the plan will be referred to as a 5-8 scheduling plan with 5 representing the number of consecutive days worked and 8 representing the number of hours worked each workday. In utilizing this plan, officers can either be assigned to permanent shifts (day, evening, or night) or rotate among the three shifts. Potential shift hours can include 7 A.M.–3 P.M., 3 P.M.–11 P.M., and 11 P.M.–7 A.M.

Benefits of 5-8 Scheduling

One of the benefits of a 5-8 scheduling plan is that it represents a traditional work schedule. Therefore, administrators are most familiar with this scheduling plan and typically feel comfortable about their level of knowledge of a 5-8 scheduling plan. In addition, officers are well adjusted to an 8-hour work day because that is what they are typically used to working regardless of their previous positions. Some officers cannot imagine working more than 8 hours in a day. Eight-hour workdays are a traditional schedule regardless of the occupation.

Another benefit of a 5-8 scheduling plan is that this type of scheduling is frequently straightforward and more convenient in comparison to some other alternatives because three 8-hour shifts divides equally into a 24-hour day. In addition, fatigue is typically not an issue with 8-hour workdays; however, it frequently becomes a significant issue when departments look at adopting alternative scheduling plans that require longer workdays.

It is argued that less fatigued officers have higher levels of productivity. Therefore, higher productivity may be a benefit of a 5-8 scheduling plan.

Another benefit of a 5-8 scheduling plan is that it provides for the shortest workday of any of the other scheduling plans. This will allow the officer to have more time each workday to spend with his/her family and to spend on recreational interests. The other scheduling plans maximize the number of days off but require longer workdays. The 5-8 scheduling plans provides for fewer days off but more time off-duty each workday. For example, if an officer works the day shift (e.g., 6 A.M.–2 P.M.), the officer will have time to pick his/her children up from school. In addition, more efficient use of equipment is another benefit of a schedule that has non-overlapping shifts.

Drawbacks of 5-8 Scheduling

One noted drawback with this scheduling plan is that officers are typically assigned permanent days off. Some of the other plans naturally allow for rotating days off. When days off are permanent, most officers will have weekdays off only and very few will have the highly coveted weekend days off. A 5-8 type of scheduling plan can be used to provide officers rotating days off but it is typically more difficult to do this using this plan in comparison to some of those discussed below.

It is also common with three 8-hour shifts to stack or hold incoming calls for service that are received late on one shift and subsequently assigned to the shift which is coming on-duty. The net result is an extended delay in the response for requests for service and a feeling among officers that they are overworked because as soon as they begin their shifts, several calls are stacked up that need an immediate response.[15]

In addition, because the shifts do not overlap, overtime expenditures are typically higher with a 5-8 scheduling plan than with other scheduling plans that allow for overlapping shifts. Furthermore, because a 5-8 scheduling plan typically involves fixed days off which are usually weekdays, court time is frequently scheduled on one of an officer's scheduled days off. With only 2 days off per week, this is more of an issue with this plan than with other plans that allow 3 days off per week. It has also been argued that with a limited amount of time off, officers have lower levels of morale and job satisfaction in comparison to officer's working in agencies utilizing other scheduling plans.

4-10 Scheduling

Under a 4-10 scheduling plan, an officer works four 10-hour days and gets 3 days off. This scheduling plan is also frequently referred to as a 4-3 schedule with 4 representing the number of consecutive days worked and 3 representing the number of consecutive days off. In this chapter, the plan will be referred to as a 4-10 scheduling plan with 4 representing the number of consecutive days worked and 10 representing the number of hours worked each workday.

Benefits of 4-10 Scheduling

One of the primary benefits of this schedule is that it allows for the over-lapping of shifts in order to increase patrol coverage during certain times of the day. Three shifts of 10 hours each day are obviously longer than a 24-hour day. Therefore, this scheduling plan allows for 6 hours of overlap. The overlap can be applied equally or unequally between shifts or can be accumulated into one period of overlap. For example, a department could equally divide the overlap among the shifts as demonstrated below.

- Day shift (6 A.M.–4 P.M.)
- Evening shift (2 P.M.–12 A.M.)
- Night shift (10 P.M.–8 A.M.)

This schedule allows 2 hours of overlap between each shift. This type of overlap may lead to another potential benefit of this type of scheduling plan which is a reduction in the need for overtime. Overtime expenditures typically occur when officers work beyond their normal shift-time for writing reports, answering calls for service, or conducting preliminary investigations. A reduction in overtime expenditures occurs because officers from an earlier shift can go to the station to finish any paperwork or other tasks while still on duty since the next shift is available to answer calls for service. In addition, this type of scheduling plan allows for more efficient shift changes because of the overlap in shifts.

As another alternative, the overlap can be accumulated into one period of overlap as demonstrated below.

- Day shift (6 A.M.–4 P.M.)
- Evening shift (4 P.M.–2 A.M.)
- Night shift (8 P.M.–6 A.M.)

The benefit of this scheduling plan is that it allows for a power shift to be formed during the highest call load times. In this example, the highest call load times are between 8 P.M. and 2 P.M.

Another benefit of a 4-10 scheduling plan is that it is seen as a suit-able compromise between 8- and 12-hour workdays. Many officers are sat-isfied with working longer shifts but are concerned that a 12-hour shift may be too tiring. Similarly, administrators may be willing to allow officers to work longer shifts but are concerned about the ability of officers to sustain a high level of productivity during a 12-hour shift.[16] Therefore, 10-hour shifts typically satisfy both officers and administrators.

In addition, a 4-10 schedule can be created where all officers on all shifts work the same day, one day a week. This day can be a high call load day when additional officers are needed or the day can also be used for special details and assignments and for in-service training. Adjusting schedules to provide training for officers is frequently a difficult task. A 4-10 schedule that assigns all patrol officers to work the same day of the week makes this task much easier. Agencies can still have their full patrol strength required for a particular shift and the remaining officers can attend training sessions. The utility of having all officers working the same day is endless.[17]

Due to favorable work hours and 3 days off each week, a 4-10 scheduling plan is expected to increase morale among officers because most officers favor this type of scheduling over 5-8 plans. In addition, it has been argued that a 4-10 scheduling plan leads to a reduction in unnecessary sick leave, stress, and fatigue among officers.[18] Furthermore, the 4-10 scheduling plan provides officers more time to pursue personal interests, spend more time with families, and become more involved in community activities because of the three consecutive days off each week. This also affords officers the opportunity to take advantage of extra duty, overtime assignments, and department-approved security jobs that may not be available with a 5-8 scheduling plan.

Drawbacks of 4-10 Scheduling

The biggest drawback of 4-10 scheduling plans is that they are typically expensive to implement. Some argue that additional personnel are needed in order to effectively implement a 4-10 scheduling plan.[19] In some instances, it has been reported that the implementation of a 4-10 scheduling plan requires a 10–20 percent increase in a department's patrol force.[20] In addition to personnel shortages, a shortage of equipment frequently occurs under this plan due to overlapping shifts. Additional vehicles, radios, shotguns, and other equipment are typically required when this scheduling plan is implemented. Many times, implementing this scheduling plan is seen more as an employee benefit than an organizational benefit because organizational costs might not be reduced, but can actually increase if more officers and equipment are needed.[21] If the patrol force is not increased, this may lead to reduced patrol coverage during periods of non-overlapping shifts.

Previously, it was noted that a 4-10 scheduling plan can lead to lower stress levels and fatigue among officers because it provides 3 consecutive days off each week. However, it has also been noted that this scheduling plan can lead to an increase in fatigue and stress due to the longer workdays. Although certainly not the responsibility of an administrator, some have argued that a drawback of 4-10 scheduling plans is that they can lead to more spending by employees for recreation and personal reasons due to more off-duty time. In addition, marital complications may increase due to spending more time together.[22]

3-12 Scheduling

Under a 3-12 scheduling plan, an officer works three (sometimes four) 12-hour days and gets 3 days off (sometimes four). This scheduling plan is also frequently referred to as a 3-3 schedule with 3 representing the number of consecutive days worked and 3 representing the number of consecutive days off. In this chapter, the plan will be referred to as a 3-12 scheduling plan with 3 representing the number of consecutive days worked and 12 representing the number of hours worked each workday.

Twelve-hour schedules are designed on the one-for-one principle: one day off for each day worked.[23]

Benefits of 3-12 Scheduling

One of the major benefits of a 3-12 scheduling plan is that it requires fewer shifts and thus fewer shift changes. Because there are only two shifts in a 3-12 scheduling plan, assuming a power shift is not used, better shift change times can be utilized. For example, under a 5-8 scheduling plan a shift change typically occurs about 10 or 11 P.M. This is usually a high call load time and can lead to the holding of calls when the shift change occurs. Under a 3-12 scheduling plan, shift changes can occur at 6 or 7 P.M. which may be a slower call time in comparison to 10 P.M. In addition, because of fewer shift changes per day there is a reduction in the number of communication errors between shifts. The officers who are coming off-duty when an officer is coming on-duty will be the same officers who will be coming on-duty when the officer is coming off-duty. This can lead to increased communication between shifts and improved continuity of operations. Furthermore, fewer shift changes per day means officers have more time on patrol.

Another benefit of a 3-12 scheduling plan is that it allows for rotating days off so each officer will experience weekends off periodically throughout the year. Off days rotate backwards 1 day every week. Off days rotate rapidly so officers have several weekends off per year (typically one weekend every month).

There are several other potential benefits of a 3-12 scheduling plan. These benefits are similar to those previously discussed for a 4-10 scheduling plan and include the following:

- Increased morale and job satisfaction (many officers like 12-hour shifts);
- More family and leisure time because more consecutive days off;
- Reduced sick leave since taking a sick day can mean a loss of 12 hours of sick time (officers will avoid taking them unless they are truly sick); and
- Fewer consecutive workdays and more rest days to dissipate fatigue.

Drawbacks of 3-12 Scheduling

A major drawback of 3-12 scheduling plans is that they seem to leave officers more fatigued, especially after the third consecutive 12-hour shift. Because 12 hours of work per day is more fatiguing than 8 hours, alertness and safety may decline as the shift progresses and officers may work at a slower pace (i.e., reduced officer productivity). An overload of stressful situations in one shift can reduce an officer's alertness and reduce an officer's willingness to be proactive when not responding to calls for service. However, one study analyzed differences in numerous physiological, psychological, and subjective measures of awareness in one police department that changed from 8- to 12-hour shifts. The results indicated no disadvantages of the schedule shift with regard to measures of alertness. In fact, the study found that 12-hour shifts may allow for greater consistency in sleep patterns and perhaps less fatigue.[24]

Overtime also becomes a significant issue with a 3-12 scheduling plan because working even 2 hours overtime leads to a 14-hour day, rather than a 10-hour day on a typical 5-8 scheduling plan. In this hypothetical 14-hour day, an officer only has 10 hours to commute, eat, spend time with his/her family, and sleep before the next shift begins. In addition, because of more consecutive days off, officers may lose touch with operations and while off, officers may be more apt to engage in off-duty security positions or other work endeavors and may return to work fatigued.

OTHER SCHEDULING ALTERNATIVES

Besides the basic scheduling plans discussed in the previous section, several scheduling alternatives are available. A few will be discussed in this section including 5-9 scheduling, overlapping shifts, power shifts, and variable start times for shifts.

5-9 Scheduling

This type of scheduling calls for an officer to work a 9-hour day for a period of 5 days. At the end of the fifth day, the officer is scheduled for either 2 or 3 consecutive days off, so the officer does not exceed the 2,080 working hours required of officers during the calendar year. This schedule provides for several periods of 3 days off in a row. With a variable number of days off each week (2 or 3), this schedule is fundamentally a rotating schedule that allows an officer far more weekend days off than characteristically experienced with 5-8 scheduling. In other words, an officer's actual days off change each week by advancing one day.[25] With this type of schedule, an officer can get 20 Saturdays, 20 Sundays, and 13 Saturday–Sunday combinations off each year.[26] If this schedule is constructed in such a way that deliberate overlapping of shifts occurs, it is possible to cover peak call and activity times with two shifts. This results in an increase in patrol strength at particular times without any increase in authorized personnel. In addition, the overlapping shifts could allow officers from the earlier shift to finish paperwork and take care of other responsibilities while the officers just coming on-duty can handle calls for service. This may lead to a reduction in overtime expenditures.

Overlapping Shifts

As demonstrated in some of the scheduling plans discussed above, one scheduling alternative is to overlap shifts in which one shift starts before the previous shift ends. This type of overlapping naturally occurs in the 4-10 and

5-9 scheduling plans previously discussed. Overlapping shifts are distinguished from power shifts, discussed below, in that the overlap between shifts is brief (typically less than one hour). The overlap time can be used for briefing or for allowing officers on the earlier shift to finish paperwork or other activities in an effort to reduce the need for overtime. Overlapping shifts are also designed to increase communication between shifts since both shifts are both on-duty at the same time, even if the time frame is brief. However, one noted problem with overlapping shifts is equipment shortages that frequently occur. The equipment shortages typically involve vehicles, radios, and other equipment used by patrol. If officers on both overlapping shifts are expected to be out on the street at the same time, then additional vehicles and other equipment are needed in comparison to shifts that do not overlap.

Power Shifts

A shift that overlaps other shifts and is substantially different from regular shift hours is called a power shift. The overlap provided by power shifts, although a form of overlapping shift, usually lasts longer than the type of overlapping shift discussed above. Typically, the overlap provided by a power shift lasts at least 4 hours in comparison to the shorter overlap previously discussed. The 4-10 scheduling plan can allow for up to a 6-hour overlapping power shift. A power shift is typically used to cover peak times for calls for service. For example, an agency may use the 5-8 scheduling plan discussed above. The shifts may be from 6 A.M. to 2 P.M., 2 P.M. to 10 P.M., and 10 P.M. to 6 A.M. Officers may be assigned to work a power shift from 6 P.M. to 2 A.M. to cover peak call load times. This type of scheduling will reduce the number of staff needed on the evening and night shift because of the overlap of officers during the busiest times in each shift.

Variable Start Times for Shifts

All officers do not need to report for work at the same time. Throughout this chapter, we have typically discussed three shifts of patrol officers per day, sometimes four with the use of power shifts. However, staggered start times for shifts can certainly be used. For example, instead of having all evening officers work 2 P.M.–10 P.M., an agency could have some of the officers come in at 2 P.M. and work until 10 P.M., some officers come in at 3 P.M. and work until 11 P.M, some officers come in at 4 P.M. and work until 12 A.M., etc. This allows for increased coverage at higher call load times but it makes scheduling more difficult and can reduce communication both within and between shifts.

SCHEDULING ISSUES

Besides making decisions regarding the best scheduling plan for a particular agency, administrators must also make decisions regarding several other scheduling issues. Issues including shift rotation, days off rotation, and proportional scheduling will be discussed in this section. Even after these decisions are made and after the work schedule has been designed and put into effect, the scheduling process is not completed or finished. In fact, it is never completed or finished. There are several day-to-day activities and decisions that impact scheduling including training, vacation and compensatory time, and administrative and unplanned absences.[27] These issues will be discussed in this section as well.

Shift Rotation

Departments typically use one of three shift rotation options: non-rotating (i.e., fixed), forward (clockwise), and backward (counterclockwise). In departments that use non-rotating shifts, officers are assigned a permanent shift typically based on seniority. The only time that shift changes occur is when a vacancy occurs in a "preferred" shift assignment because either a more senior officer has been reassigned to another division within the department (e.g., investigations) or an officer retires. Therefore, once an officer is assigned a particular shift, the shift remains the same.

Many departments rotate their shifts and require officers to work all shifts for certain periods of time. In forward (clockwise) rotation, the shift rotation pattern follows the clock, from days, to evenings, to nights. In backward (counterclockwise) rotation, the shift rotation moves against the clock, from days, to nights, to evenings. Overall, it is argued that forward rotation is the easiest to adapt to from a physiological standpoint. It takes about 8 days for an officer to adjust to a forward rotation (e.g., from evening shift to night shift), but it takes about 12 days for an officer to adjust to a backward rotation (e.g., from day shift to night shift).[28]

The number of off-duty hours provided between shift changes should be sufficient to allow the officer to adjust to the new hours and to provide adequate rest before returning to duty. It is difficult, if not impossible, for an officer to adequately adjust to a new shift if the officer rotating from days to nights is expected to report to both in the same day. In other words, it is ineffective to make officers who finished the day shift at 2 P.M. to report back to the night shift at 10 P.M. that same day because the officer is rotating to nights. Off-duty periods of less than 16 hours at a shift change are considered short changeovers and can be avoided with some schedules.[29]

In departments that rotate shifts, the length of time spent on each shift varies. The lengths on each shift may vary from weekly, to monthly, to quarterly, to semi-annually, to yearly. Overall, longer lengths of time between shift rotations are preferable to allow an officer enough time to physiologically adjust to the new shift before being switched again. Some studies have argued that the minimum shift rotation should occur no less than every three weeks.[30] Many departments also rotate days off at shift change to give every officer an opportunity to have a weekend off periodically.

In making a decision about whether shifts should be fixed or rotated, police administrators should take several factors into account.

For example, if an agency places significant emphasis on its patrol officers performing community policing activities, fixed shifts may facilitate community policing efforts better than rotating shifts. This is especially true when shift rotation occurs rapidly. In addition, if shifts are not rotated periodically, more senior officers will occupy the morning shift which will leave the less experienced officers on the night shift. Some departments require that a certain percentage of each shift consists of senior officers to overcome this issue.[31] Furthermore, if an agency wants to facilitate an officer's desire to obtain a baccalaureate or postbaccalaureate degree, then shifts should be either fixed or rotated to coincide with semester furloughs. In other words, rotating from evenings to days may interfere with the educational schedule of officers taking day classes. The ability to adapt to rotating shifts declines with age and should be taken into consideration by administrators in determining what is best for their agency.

The question then becomes, which is better, shift rotation or permanent shift assignments? Obviously, the question cannot be universally answered but must be answered by each individual agency. It is important that administrators recognize that this issue evokes strong feelings and opinions among officers because it affects both their work environment as well as their personal habits and their family life.

From a scheduling standpoint, a fixed shift system is simplest. Everyone knows which shift they are assigned to, and extra effort does not need to be placed on figuring out an effective means to rotate shifts. In addition, some officers prefer a fixed shift system even when they are not on the day shift. Some officers prefer days, some evenings, and some nights. Having fixed shifts may allow officers to work in the shift that they most prefer. It also allows them to adjust to the physical, emotional, and social demands of a particular shift.[32] In addition, when based on seniority, it is seen as an enticement and reward for staying with the department. Problems have been noted with this practice, however. Some of the problems discussed include reduced productivity over time because officers become stale working the same shift and reduced communication between personnel assigned to various shifts.[33]

Obviously, not all officers prefer a fixed shift system, but instead would opt for a rotating system. Newer officers may believe that a fixed shift system, especially one based on seniority, is unfair because they are typically left with the night shift until they gain enough experience and seniority to obtain a more preferred shift. Some officers do not feel that seniority is a good enough reason for allowing such preferred shift assignments because they are doing the same type and level of work as officers with more seniority. These officers prefer a rotating shift system in which all officers are required to work all the shifts at some time.[34] In addition, officers who prefer variety and change may like rotating shift systems because actual police operations vary by type depending on the time of day. Therefore, by rotating shifts, officers are exposed to a wider range of job functions than may be available in a fixed shift system.[35] However, some problems with shift rotation have been noted previously. These problems include disruption of outside education and employment commitments, problems with family life, and fatigue from short off-duty periods when changing from one shift to another.[36]

Days Off Rotation

Another issue that is similar to shift rotation is whether days off should be rotated or fixed. When days off are permanent or fixed, most officers will typically have weekdays off only and very few will have the highly coveted weekend days off. The 5-8 and 4-10 scheduling plans discussed in the chapter typically require fixed days off. However, these plans can be modified to provide for rotating days off. As previously discussed, the 3-12 scheduling plan allows for rotating days off. Some officers favor fixed days off because they find it easier to schedule educational and recreational activities. However, some officers do not like the monotony of having the same days off each week, and some supervisors argue that fixed days off do not expose officers to varying service conditions that may exist on different days of the week.[37] In addition, most officers would like to occasionally have a weekend off, which is typically only reserved for the most senior officers when days off are fixed.

Usually, it is difficult to have fixed days off along with rotating shift assignments because of poor changeover properties that are usually encountered when rotating from one shift to another. However, this issue can partially be remedied by extending the length of time between shift rotations.[38]

Proportional Scheduling

Some law enforcement agencies provide uniform staffing levels across all shifts and days of week even though calls for service vary by shift and day of week. This practice is known as non-proportional scheduling. The problems with non-proportional scheduling include excessive fatigue for the officers who work busier shifts without additional personnel, lower morale, inefficient use of personnel and equipment, greater overtime on busier shifts, increased response times on busier shifts, and officer boredom during low call load times.[39]

To overcome these issues, law enforcement agencies frequently schedule their officers proportionally based on workload experienced by time of day and day of week. More officers are scheduled to work during high workload times and fewer are scheduled during low workload times. Thus, proportional scheduling involves assigning a different number of officers during different times of the day and different days of the weeks. In other words, a different number of officers will be assigned to the day, evening, and night shifts. In addition, a different number of officers will be assigned for each day of the week within the same shift. For example, 10 officers may be assigned to work on Tuesday evenings, but 13 may be assigned to work on Friday evenings.

In proportional scheduling, departments typically use calls for service by time of day and day of week when making scheduling decisions. As an example, if 50 percent of the calls for service occur during the evening shift, then 50 percent of the patrol officers are assigned to the evening shift. Similarly, if 25 percent of the calls for service occur during the day shift and 25 percent during the night shift, then the remaining patrol force is scheduled equally on these two shifts. Proportional scheduling makes good management sense because it provides better coverage than scheduling an equal number of officers for each shift, and it can save resources as well.

However, it is important to note that scheduling based on the number of calls for service by time of day and day of week does not always accurately reflect what officers do on an actual shift. In other words, as noted in the previous chapter, officers do more than just answering calls for service. Officers are responsible for meeting various performance objectives set by agency administrators and for spending adequate time conducting self-initiated or directed patrol activities. For example, in a particular agency there may be fewer calls for service on the night shift. In proportional scheduling based on calls for service, this would necessitate fewer officers being scheduled for the night shift in comparison to the day and evening shift. However, an agency may want their officers to provide more security checks of businesses and residences during the night shift which, thus, takes up a greater proportion of officers' time in comparison to the other two shifts. In addition, certain calls for service may take longer or require more back-up than calls for service that occur during the day. For example, accidents may take longer for officers to work on the night shift because of the more limited visibility of other motorists at night in comparison to the day. This would require more officers to control traffic flow around the accident scene at night. Or perhaps it is recognized that accidents that occur at night are typically more serious and thus take more time to investigate. In addition, it may be recognized that calls for service, in general, on the night shift tend to be more serious and thus take more time to handle. The point is that administrators need to recognize these differences between shifts and make scheduling adjustments where necessary to take into consideration the uniqueness of each shift rather than just the number of calls for service on each shift.

In order to overcome problems associated with matching the number of officers on a shift with demand for service, some departments establish minimum staffing levels for each shift during the week. When insufficient personnel are available to meet a shift minimum (because of sick or injury leave, unexpected special assignment, or any other unplanned absence), agencies have put in place several procedures that should be followed in order to meet minimum staffing levels. These procedures include temporarily reassigning on-duty officers from other shifts with more than the minimum number of on-duty personnel, designating officers to serve as floaters or relief personnel to cover shortages, holding officers beyond their assigned work shift, and calling back off-duty officers.[40]

Scheduling Training

Training time is at a premium in most agencies and is frequently difficult to manage from a scheduling perspective. Some departments schedule training during officers' days off that requires the department to pay overtime to officers for training. Some scheduling plans provide an abundance of training time built in the schedule. This allows officers to attend training during regular work hours and at no extra cost to the department. For example, some departments schedule all patrol officers to work a particular day of the week (e.g., Wednesday). Because of the abundance of officers assigned on that one day, several officers can be assigned to participate in training sessions without reducing the normal level of actual on-duty personnel.

Scheduling Vacation and Compensatory Time

Vacation time is typically computed as a specified number of on-duty shifts, on-duty hours, or calendar days (with no regard for the number of on-duty assignments during that time).[41] Departments attempt to administer vacation time efficiently and fairly through policies, procedures, and the exercise of supervisory judgment. However, a number of problems frequently occur with scheduling vacation time. First, staffing levels are frequently difficult to maintain during popular vacation times. Most officers would like to take their vacation time in the summer, but appropriate staffing levels must be maintained year round in order to effectively provide police services to the community. If too many officers are allowed to take vacation at one time, this can lead to excessive overtime expenditures when unforeseen or unexpected absences occur during popular vacation times. Second, seniority is frequently used to determine the distribution of vacation times which means that only senior officers get to take vacation time in the summer.[42]

It may seem surprising that this annual fringe benefit can cause such problems with scheduling, but it does. Many departments have extensive vacation policies that dictate procedures for assuring adequate staffing levels during vacation times, maintaining staffing levels during vacation periods in the event of emergency/unforeseen conditions, establishing periods of the year when vacation can be taken, combining vacation time with other forms of time off such as compensatory time, identifying vacation selection procedures, and requesting and approving vacation time.[43] Administrators in charge of scheduling must be able to adapt the schedule to accommodate vacation time for officers.

Although not typically taken in significant blocks of time (e.g., 5 consecutive days), the use of compensatory (comp) time by officers can have a significant impact on scheduling. Typically, comp time is allowed to accrue until 8 hours (when 8-hour shifts are used) or more has been accumulated. After that time, an officer may request to take a day off with supervisory approval. In some police departments, the process of scheduling comp time becomes routine, with certain days of the week in which comp time off can be taken.[44] These days of the week are typically days with a lighter work-load or days in which all officers are scheduled for duty (as was discussed above in regards to scheduling training time). Scheduling vacation and comp time further complicates the scheduling process.

Administrative and Unplanned Absences

Administrative and unplanned absences contribute to personnel shortages and therefore can negatively impact work schedules as well. Adminis-trative absences can include court time (either while on-duty or on the offi-cer's time off, but then compensated for by time-off taken later), military leave, special assignments, educational leave to attend school or advanced training, disciplinary action, and limited duty time (when officer is recover-ing from an injury). Unplanned absences include sick leave and personal emergency leave. Whether planned or unplanned, these absences can add up to a significant amount of time each year.[45] It is important to keep records of these absences in order to attempt to predict, whenever possible, their occurrence so that steps can be taken to lessen their impact on staffing levels.

CONCLUSION

Although this chapter has focused on patrol scheduling, it is important to note that alternative work schedules can be developed for all divisions within a police department. For example, it might be decided that it is best that patrol resources be scheduled on a 4-10 schedule. The overlap of offi-cers coming on- and off-duty can be arranged to cover peak periods for calls for service. Therefore, shift hours may be arranged from 6 A.M. to 4 P.M., 4 P.M. to 2 A.M., and 8 P.M. to 6 A.M.

For administrative positions (captains, deputy chiefs, and chiefs), a traditional 5-8 schedule may work best to conform to other city services and administrators. These positions would operate on a traditional work-week schedule (8 A.M.–5 P.M. Monday through Friday). At the same time, a 10- or 12-hour schedule might suit a detective division best because it can reduce overtime costs when detectives are scheduled 8 A.M.–5 P.M. Obviously, detectives are often required to interview people after 5 P.M., and extending the shift to 10 or 12 hours allows this type of activity to occur more readily without overtime expenditures. A traffic division may be most effectively deployed on a 12-hour schedule so they can be out on the street during the morning rush hour and remain on-duty through the evening rush hour (e.g., 6:30 A.M.–6:30 P.M.). Similarly, officers assigned as school resource officers should probably be assigned to 5-8 schedules so they are available from Monday through Friday when school is open. Therefore, a police agency will probably use several varieties of the scheduling plans presented in this chapter because of the varied nature of police work.

ENDNOTES

1. W. W. Stenzel and R. M. Buren, *Police Work Scheduling: Management Issues and Practices* (Washington, D.C.: U.S. Department of Justice, 1983).
2. Ibid.
3. Ibid.
4. Ibid.
5. B. Vila, G. B. Morrison, and D. J. Kenney, "Improving Shift Schedule and Work-Hour Policies and Practices to Increase Police Officer Performance, Health, and Safety." *Police Quarterly* 5, no. 1 (2002): 4–24.
6. Ibid.
7. Ibid.
8. Ibid.
9. Stenzel and Buren, *Police Work Scheduling*.
10. Ibid.
11. W. L. Booth, *Manager's Guide to Alternative Work Schedules*, 2nd ed. (Jacksonville, FL: Institute of Police Technology and Management, 1989).
12. Ibid.
13. Stenzel and Buren, *Police Work Scheduling*.
14. Ibid., 201.
15. D. Dalton, H. C. Heyen, and M. Whitemeyer, "The '9-5' Plan: An Alternative to '10-4' Plans that Works." *The Police Chief* 45, December 1978.
16. Booth, *Manager's Guide to Alternative Work Schedules*.
17. Ibid.
18. Dalton et al., "The '9-5' Plan."
19. Ibid.
20. Ibid.
21. Booth, *Manager's Guide to Alternative Work Schedules*.
22. G. E. Ward, "The '9-40' Plan: Manpower Deployment and Shift Scheduling for Small and Medium Sized Police Department." *The Police Chief* 45, December 1978.
23. Booth, *Manager's Guide to Alternative Work Schedules*.
24. B. Peacock, R. Glube, M. Miller, and P. Clune, "Police Officers' Responses to 8 and 12 Hour Shift Schedules." *Ergonomics* 26, no. 5 (1983): 479–93.
25. Dalton et al., "The '9-5' Plan."
26. Ibid.
27. Stenzel and Buren, *Police Work Scheduling*.
28. Vila et al., "Improving Shift Schedule and Work-Hour Policies and Practices to Increase Police Officer Performance, Health, and Safety."
29. Stenzel and Buren, *Police Work Scheduling*.
30. J. Lawrence, "Patrol Scheduling Methods in Texas Police Agencies." *TELEMASP Bulletin* 2, no. 4 (July 1995): 1–8.
31. Ibid.
32. Booth, *Manager's Guide to Alternative Work Schedules*.
33. Stenzel and Buren, *Police Work Scheduling*.
34. Booth, *Manager's Guide to Alternative Work Schedules*.
35. Ibid.
36. Stenzel and Buren, *Police Work Scheduling*.
37. Ibid.
38. Ibid.
39. Ibid.
40. Ibid.
41. Ibid.
42. Ibid.
43. Ibid.
44. Ibid.
45. Ibid.

6

Deployment and the Emergence of Modern Tactics

This chapter covers concrete programs, tactics, and behaviors that we refer to as "modern tactical deployment approaches." Specific tactics that are discussed include (1) directed patrol, (2) "hot spot" patrol, and (3) aggressive patrol and "zero-tolerance" tactics. Although there are certainly similarities between these tactics, they will be discussed separately. In addition, most police agencies engage in all of these tactics in certain areas and under certain circumstances. Furthermore, this chapter will cover the three primary deployment models used in law enforcement agencies today.

DIRECTED PATROL

Directed patrol was initially developed by officers of the Kansas City, MO Police Department in the mid-1970s.[1] The primary goal of directed patrol is the reduction of specific crimes, for example, residential burglary or armed robbery, in a given geographical location. According to this tactic, officers are "directed" to patrol a specific location for a specific period of time in an attempt to apprehend or deter specific criminal types. Patrol officers are directed to spend some of their patrol time in certain areas, to adopt certain tactics, and/or to watch for particular types of offenses. Directed patrol requires that a department move away from allowing calls for service to dominate patrol officer shift time and toward a model where problems are analyzed and strategic plans drive patrol operations.[2] Patrol planners in Kansas City estimated that as much as one-third of all patrol time could be devoted to directed patrol. Thus, a substantial portion of officers could logically be transferred from routine patrol to directed patrols.

Directed patrol projects share four common elements: (1) Directed patrol is proactive and aggressive; (2) Directed patrol officers use noncommitted time to engage in purposeful law enforcement activity; (3) Directed patrol units have specific instructions directing their activities; and (4) The instructions (directions) are based on thorough analyses of crime data.[3] Several studies have supported the idea that crime can be specifically reduced by directing officers to crime targets. Following implementation of crime analysis and directed patrol in one community, Part I crimes (i.e., murder, rape, robbery, aggravated assault, burglary, motor vehicle theft, theft, and arson) were reduced by approximately 25 percent.[4] In 1973, the Denver Police Department implemented the High Impact Anti-Crime Program and developed a unique version of directed patrol called the Special Crime Attack Team (SCAT). A key component of SCAT was that the officers were trained in community relations to avoid antagonizing the residents. The unit employed three major strategies: prevention, interception, and investigation—however, specific emphasis was placed on contacting members of the community and business groups whenever they were going to target an area and also provided free security checks in an effort to increase police–community relations while working on solving the problems the team targeted. SCAT employed a variety of tactics that included undercover operations, stakeouts, plain clothes patrol, and saturation patrol. The program eventually targeted seven neighborhoods, which included eleven different precincts in Denver. Pre-/post-comparison statistics revealed that burglary decreased 18.5 percent and aggravated robbery 15.5 percent from the previous year in the targeted areas.[5]

Three cities, Albuquerque, NM; Charlotte, NC; and Sacramento, CA, were selected in 1978 to implement and field-test a directed patrol program. The program in Charlotte focused on redirecting resource allocation and formalizing directed patrol. Directed patrol in Charlotte meant that some patrol assignments would take priority over calls for service. The units on directed patrol would only be interrupted to respond to emergency calls for service. Directed patrol assignments included decoy operations, stakeouts, and simply increasing presence through visibility in certain areas of the city.[6] The process of identifying targets for directed patrol was formalized and supervised by agency administrators.[7] Under this plan, communication between command, crime analysis, and field officers was increased. The evaluation found that target offenses decreased in 16 out of 23 (70 percent) directed patrol activities. The average decrease in offenses was 28 percent.[8] Although these results were promising, the findings were interpreted cautiously because the study failed to account for other factors that could have produced the offense declines, and issues concerning the degree to which these crimes were simply displaced to other areas were not addressed. Although the programs in Albuquerque and Sacramento were slightly different, similar offense reductions occurred.[9] Additionally, several other studies using simple pre-/post-comparisons found similar results,[10] while other studies found that directed patrol programs had limited or no impact.[11]

The New Haven, CT Police Department began a directed patrol experiment in 1976, primarily because department executives concluded that patrol units were not well positioned to prevent crime during uncommitted time.[12] The program sought to reallocate uncommitted time in between dispatches without undergoing a major reorganization. The stated goal of the program was deterrence rather than criminal apprehension, specifically deterrence of suppressible crimes only.[13] These included auto theft, purse snatchings, commercial burglaries, and residential burglaries. Using crime analysis data, a series of directed patrol pattern sheets (D-runs) were prepared, with between 5 and 10 percent of the D-runs being replaced each month. Anywhere from thirty to thirty-five D-runs were distributed to officers on each shift. The patrol officers were given no schedule for the D-runs. Instead, they were advised by dispatch when to begin a directed patrol run.[14]

D-runs were given the same priority as a call for service—the D-run had to be completed before a unit was placed back into service. Analysis revealed that 83 percent of the D-runs were completed. In the year following the implementation of the program, residential burglaries decreased by 16 percent, commercial burglaries 8 percent, auto thefts 6 percent, and purse snatchings 9 percent. There were also reductions in thefts from autos and vandalism as well, even though these offenses were not targeted. The program contained three important, interrelated components: (1) identification through rigorous crime analysis of the places and times when crimes had occurred, (2) preparation of written directions that described in detail the way problem areas were to be patrolled, and (3) the determination of activation time of these patrol directions by crime analysis.[15]

In the late 1970s, Pontiac, MI, experimented with directed patrol as part of the federally funded Integrated Criminal Apprehension Program.[16] Over a period of nearly one and a half years, directed patrol responsibilities were shifted from all patrol personnel to a special directed patrol unit, and subsequently switched back over to a division-wide approach. The study concluded that target crimes could be decreased through the use of directed patrol based on crime analysis. Interestingly, in Pontiac the most significant impact was achieved during the initial time period when directed patrol assignments were widely distributed among all patrol officers. Overly large investments of time in limited areas, however, appeared to offer no additional effects, perhaps because of the relatively small number of "opportunities" in any particular target area for aggressive patrol efforts.[17]

For almost 30 weeks, the Kansas City Police Department increased directed patrols in gun crime hot spots in the Central Patrol District. In the target area, officers were freed from calls for service and focused on gun detection through proactive directed patrol activities. Four officers worked six hours of overtime (7 P.M. to 1 A.M.) for 176 nights, and two other officers worked an additional 24 nights for a total of 4,512 officer hours and 2,256 patrol car hours. The gun seizures were typically the result of searches and frisks that followed arrests on other charges. The evaluation team rode along with the unit for 300 hours of observation, and the targeted area was compared to a control area that had experienced similar levels of violent crime and drive-by shootings.[18]

The results showed that officers on directed patrol spent 30 percent of their time actually on patrol, thus 70 percent of their time was spent on arrests and other processing activities. In the target area, 65 percent more guns were seized in the second half of 1992 than were seized in the first half (46 compared with 76, respectively). In the comparison area where the level of patrol was not changed, gun seizures decreased over the same time period. As a result, gun crimes in the targeted area were reduced by 49 percent. In addition, drive-by shootings dropped from 7 to 1 in the target area, while they increased from 6 to 12 in the comparison area. No displacement was found, and when the patrols were ceased, gun crimes in the target area gradually increased until the program was reinstituted and gun crimes reduced once again. Only gun-related crimes were affected by the directed patrols, and the results showed that the directed patrols were three times more cost effective in getting guns off the streets when compared to regular patrol.[19]

HOT SPOT PATROL

One area of patrol research that has recently received substantial attention is hot spot patrol. The idea of crime "hot spots" was introduced by Sherman, Gartin, and Buerger[20] who found that substantial concentrations of all police calls—especially those related to serious violent crime—are concentrated in relatively few "hot spots," or small geographic areas that produce a large number of calls for service. In fact, this research found that 50.4 percent of all calls to the Minneapolis Police Department were concentrated in only 3.3 percent of all addresses and roadway intersections in the city.[21] The "hot spot" pattern was consistent for a wide range of crime types, including those that were committed indoors. The concentration of calls for service in the hot spots was significantly greater than that would be expected by chance alone, and the hot spots produced large numbers of both predatory crime calls and total calls. In addition, hot spots were often clustered within one or two blocks of one another. The results of this research were confirmed by replications in Kansas City and Boston.[22] The Kansas City study and other subsequent research led to the concept of intensive patrolling of these high-crime "hot spots."

In the 1987 Minneapolis Repeat Call Address Policing (RECAP) Experiment, patrol officers were given directed assignments that called for problem-solving at locations that had been identified as requiring frequent police services. The idea was to solve the problems that generated repeat calls, thereby reducing the volume of activity at those addresses. The officers involved in the project were formed into special teams. Each team participated in location-specific call analyses, the design of tactics for reducing the volume of calls, as well as the implementation of chosen tactics.

The RECAP project showed considerable success after 6 months as calls for service that were derived from the experimental addresses were reduced significantly. However, during the subsequent 6 months, officers increasingly found their targets resistant to further improvement. In fact, by the fourth quarter of the project, all of the earlier results had disappeared. From the researcher's perspective, the obvious conclusion was that an operational policy of short-term targeting might offer the best investment of police resources. Instead of attempting to maintain a tactical response over a long period of time, departments should alter their tactics by constantly changing crackdown targets, and thereby reduce crime through residual deterrence. Moreover, the tactic of constantly altering the focus of hot spot crackdowns could work to save resources that would otherwise be wasted on patrols that would suffer from diminished returns over time.[23]

In a related study, Koper[24] tested whether or not hot spot patrols produced residual deterrence on disorderly behavior (rather than more serious crime). He found that stronger doses of patrol (i.e., longer duration of time at the hot spot) improved the residual deterrence of criminal and disorderly behavior at the hot spots. He also found through survival analysis that the optimum time was about 14 or 15 minutes—10 minutes was the minimum and after 20 minutes the returns from continued presence diminished.[25] The implications are clear—police can maximize the reduction of serious crime *and* disorder by spending the optimal amount of time at particular hot spots.

Several other replications and extensions of the hot spots research have been conducted. The Kansas City Gun Experiment used hot spots of gun crime activity to focus a small number of police officers on the goal of producing gun seizures. The results showed a significant reduction in gun-related crime in target areas without displacement.[26] Further, hot spot policing was found to be effective in reducing emergency calls in drug markets[27] and in reducing crime around crack houses.[28] One study found no displacement[29] while the other found that raids on crack houses showed a significant effect on the overall crime rate; however, the effects decayed quickly and crime returned.[30] To date, the research on hot spots is undoubtedly the most well-designed, well-conceived test of police patrol on crime available. In addition, the results were replicated across jurisdictions and varying types of crime with similar significant reductions in crime, disorder, and calls for service being noted.

The revelation that a very small percentage of addresses account for a disproportionate amount of serious crime—a fact that most patrol officers could already attest to from their "non-scientific" but authentic experience on the street—has produced some major implications for those charged with directing patrol resources. First, police executives should strive to target these hot spot areas for active intervention rather than deploy consistent patrol levels across particular beats or sectors. Second, the research concerning the effectiveness of hot spot patrols provides further evidence that proactive and aggressive strategies can work if they are properly focused on specific places and/or targets.[31] The strategy for police executives seems clear: identify the hot spots through crime analysis, focus patrol resources on those hot spots, and subsequently evaluate the results regarding calls for service and crime that those hot spots produce.

AGGRESSIVE PATROL AND ZERO-TOLERANCE TACTICS

A more traditional response to crime problems is an approach that is alternately referred to as "aggressive patrol" or patrols that employ "zero-tolerance" tactics against particular types of crime. Essentially, these types of strategies involve a high level of patrol intervention through traffic stops, minor offense enforcement, and field interrogations (FIs) of people on the street to reduce incidences of street crime.[32] Some research concludes that cities with more aggressive patrol tactics have had lower robbery rates.[33] The crime reduction accomplishments associated with aggressive patrols and zero-tolerance tactics appear to result from more frequent traffic stops and field interrogations rather than simple increases in time spent in particular areas.[34] That is, these strategies have more to do with *what* officers do on patrol than *how much* time they spend on particular tasks or in particular places.

Several experimental and quasi-experimental research studies have found that aggressive repeat offender programs (ROP) have yielded significant results in both increasing the likelihood of arrest, conviction, and punishment of repeat offenders as well as reducing crime.[35] These programs aggressively target repeat offenders for street-level patrol intervention. A twenty-one person special patrol unit of the Louisiana State Troopers was trained in a criminal patrol techniques school, and, in 45 days, the unit made 345 criminal arrests.[36] The arrests were not solely for minor traffic offenses or petty misdemeanor crimes, but rather they included arrests of fugitives wanted for murder, child abuse, drug trafficking, and auto theft. Additionally, the experience raised morale among the patrol officers who participated in the program.[37]

In an experimental test in San Diego, eliminating the use of FIs led to crime increases, whereas re-instituting FIs resulted in crime decreases.[38] For a 9-month period, the levels of field interrogation activity were manipulated: the *no-FI beat* had all FI activity eliminated; the *control beat* retained a "normal" level of FI activity (about 20 per month); and the *special FI beat* received extra FI activity (almost 50 per month).[39] The study found that suppressible crime increased significantly (by 39 percent) in areas where field interrogations were discontinued. Once the FIs were resumed, these same crimes returned to approximately their previous levels.[40] This apparent FI effect was not simply a mask for an arrest effect, since arrests in the no-FI area actually increased by about 25 percent during the experimental period. In other words, the level of suppressible crime appeared to have been affected by the use or avoidance of field interrogations, independent of the number of arrests made in the area.[41]

Aggressive policing strategies were also evaluated in sixty residential neighborhoods in three cities, Rochester, NY; St. Louis, MO; and Tampa/St. Petersburg, FL. The patrol officers used four distinct forms of aggressive tactics including officer-initiated suspicion stops, officer-initiated investigatory activities (warrantless searches, crime scene inspections, and questioning potential witnesses beyond the immediate scene), residential security checks, and proactive order maintenance activities. The study found that the most effective tactic was the level of officer-initiated suspicion stops. The effect was most prominent on auto theft and vandalism; however, this effect was not as stable as the effect on robbery.[42]

Several additional studies have also found differences in crime levels when using aggressive patrol tactics.[43] Skogan[44] concluded that police efforts in several cities where intensive enforcement was used were not effective in reducing social disorder. However, when statistics from the research are examined, the reductions in areas where intensive enforcement was used were as strong as other techniques, and the findings were significant.

Zero-tolerance tactics and other types of what Sherman[45] refers to as "crackdown" tactics became quite widespread in the 1980s, particularly in response to drunk driving, public drug markets, street-walking prostitutes, and even illegal parking. Likewise, implementation of the Compstat model in New York City, which will be discussed in chapter 7, was accompanied by the use of zero-tolerance approaches to combat street prostitution, drug dealing, and other disorderly offenses.[46] For example, New York City officers began to target "squeegee gangs" that had created problems when they continually confronted motorists with aggressive demands for money in exchange for the unsolicited cleaning of car windows.[47] Houston Police increased attention on what the FBI refers to as less serious "Part II" offenses such as simple assault, vice crimes, and vandalism. Zero tolerance tactics not only reduced these types of offenses, but also coincided in a major reduction of more serious crimes.[48] For example, increased arrests for curfew, DUI, and misdemeanor assaults corresponded to decreases in Part 1 offenses, specifically suppressible street crimes such as robbery, burglary, and auto theft.

Finally, gangs and gang-related crimes have often been the target of zero-tolerance approaches. Traditional law enforcement activities designed to deal with gangs rely on sweeps and increased arrests.[49] Suppression approaches are loosely based on deterrence principles and in regards to gangs can be manifested most typically by street sweeps, special gang probation and parole caseloads, prosecutions programs, various civil procedures, and school programs.[50] Police suppression tactics targeting gangs are extensive and, sometimes, very creative.[51] Several authors, while noting that gangs probably cannot be eradicated, believe that the police can manage and, in effect, suppress the more negative aspects of gang activity.[52] These claims aside, the effectiveness of zero-tolerance approaches to gang activity has not been systematically evaluated.[53] In fact, some evaluative statements are based on hunches because of the lack of empirical data. For example, Klein[54] states, "my informed hunch is that suppression programs, left to their own devices, may deter a few members but also increase the internal cohesiveness of the group." In short, the increased attention may provide the gang members with the status and recognition that they seek. Indeed, the bulk of the current literature concludes that traditional law enforcement tactics alone will have little effect on reducing, managing, or suppressing gangs.[55]

The effect of zero-tolerance approaches to curfew and truancy on gang-related crime was analyzed in Dallas, TX. A quasi-experimental design was employed to assess the impact of an antigang initiative performed by Dallas Police.[56] The main objective of the initiative was to decrease gang-related violence in five targeted patrol areas. The study found a statistically significant decrease (57 percent) in gang-related violence in the target areas during the study period. Statistically significant decreases in gang violence were observed in the control areas during the antigang initiative as well, but the overall decrease was less substantial than the target areas; 37 percent in the control areas in comparison to 57 percent in the target areas. Geographic displacement was controlled for and was not judged to be a problem.[57] Of the documented strategies used in each area, the vast majority of overtime hours were spent on curfew enforcement in target area 1 (80 percent of overtime hours) and truancy enforcement in target areas 4 and 5 (89 percent of overtime hours). Therefore, concentrated efforts by patrol to enforce truancy and curfew laws had a positive impact on reducing gang violence.

These findings aside, police executives need to recognize the dangers associated with enacting aggressive patrols and zero-tolerance tactics. Specifically, there are problems related to moving from a purely reactive model of patrol to one that is predominately proactive and more aggressive, especially in terms of confronting citizens as targets in these new approaches. Some advocates of these aggressive patrol strategies appear to advocate a nostalgic return to the days of "non-legalistic ass-kicking," whereby officers used their discretion to physically dominate citizens and control their beat without concern to individual rights.[58] Can historically corruptible police departments prevent officers from abusing their newly found authority and mitigate concerns that officers will discriminate against certain segments of the population? The increased level of police interventions that is inherent in zero-tolerance and aggressive tactics may not always be appreciated, especially by those people who are stopped and temporarily detained.[59] Such dissatisfaction may be minimized if police are skillful in picking out truly suspicious people and in persuading people of the legitimacy of aggressive police actions;[60] however, citizen complaints may be an inevitable by-product of these tactics.

DEPLOYMENT MODELS

In order to effectively implement the modern tactical deployment approaches discussed above, agencies typically adopt one of three deployment models. This section will cover the three primary deployment models used in law enforcement agencies today.

Model 1—Overlay Deployment Model

In the overlay deployment model, agencies continue to deploy patrol officers who respond to calls for service and use uncommitted patrol time for proactive, self-initiated enforcement efforts. As an overlay to these regular patrol units, specialist officers engage in other responsibilities including, but not limited to, structured community contact and problem solving, gang enforcement, school initiatives, criminal investigation, and traffic enforcement. For example, a community resource officer can be assigned to some aggregation of regular patrol beats, work a flexible schedule, not answer calls for service, and hypothetically provide support to regular patrol through community engagement and problem solving.

Recently, agencies have created Crime Response Teams (CRTs), or some other named unit, that is a group of officers, separated from regular patrol duties, that is designed to focus on particular crime problems in the community. CRTs typically employ the deployment tactics, previously discussed, such as hot spot policing and zero-tolerance tactics to target exacerbating crime problems. However, CRTs can be allocated and deployed based on several tactics, but the question still remains, how many units of this type are needed? The commitment to using CRTs must be gauged based on the crime problems present and the need to respond to crime problems quickly. CRTs require timely crime analysis and clear tactics to be used most effectively. In essence, they should be used as the heart of the crime interdiction effort—coordinating departmental resources and information to be used for crime interdiction efforts. The research shows that directed tactics are more effective than simple visibility.

The amount of specialization within the agency is largely dependent on the size of the agency. Moderate-to-large sized agencies have more ability to specialize and implement the overlay model than small agencies. The overlay model does not preclude the enforcement of particular crimes by regular patrol officers. Rather, use of the model reflects an increased emphasis on the part of police administrators to mitigate specific problems in the jurisdiction related to such things as gangs, traffic, and school-related matters.

Model 2—Generalist Deployment Model

A second model is the generalist deployment model. Using this scheme, patrol is staffed at a level sufficient that officers can not only meet the responsibilities for responding to calls for service and proactive enforcement but also engage in structured community contact and problem solving, traffic enforcement, a moderate amount of criminal investigation, and other responsibilities. This is the typical deployment model used in small agencies due to a lack of personnel needed to specialize under the overlay deployment model. More than 75 percent of the local police agencies in the United States have less than 25 officers.[61] These agencies may have a few full-time investigators, but the rest of the line personnel are assigned to patrol as generalists.

While use of the generalist model is most common among the smallest agencies, the model has also been utilized by medium-sized and larger departments that want to apply additional patrol responsibilities beyond those related specifically to responding to citizen calls. For example, some agencies have utilized a generalist deployment model with the implementation of community policing. In these agencies, instead of assigning a group of officers to a specialized community policing unit, the adage that "every officer is a community policing officer" applies. Under these circumstances, it is assumed that there will be sufficient patrol staffing so that some flexibility exists in relieving officers from the immediate responsibility for calls for service response during periods of a shift, or at least during a period of a month in order to participate in community policing activities. The "every officer is a community policing officer" concept seems attractive since it engages all personnel in the agency and avoids the relegation of structured community policing to a specialist role. But questions must be asked of this concept as well.

- Does any community policing really occur?
- Is this any more than politically correct rhetoric?
- How can officers use unpredictable and uneven segments of uncommitted patrol time to engage in either structured community contact or problem solving?

Agencies have also experimented with expanding the role of patrol officers in criminal investigation after studies demonstrated the importance of the preliminary investigation on solving cases. Expanding the role and responsibilities of patrol officers in criminal investigation is illustrative of the generalist deployment model.

Model 3—Geographic/Sector Deployment Model

This deployment model is largely a response to two organizational realities that were the direct results of professional era reforms. One primary objective of professional era reforms was to curb rampant corruption committed by patrol officers at the beat level. During the late nineteenth century and extending into much of the twentieth century, beat officers were notorious for being "on the take," or receiving payoffs from local crime bosses in exchange for the non-enforcement of gambling, prostitution, and other forms of vice crime. Prior to reform, patrol officers were typically assigned to permanent beat assignments, a situation that was thought to encourage rampant corruption by creating long-standing relationships between officers and members of the professional underworld.[62] Professional era reformers sought to sever these ties by instituting rotational beat assignments, and most large police agencies had implemented this strategy by the 1960s.

A second primary strategy of professional era reform was to increasingly subdivide police agencies into specialized units, particularly the creation of plainclothes detective units. These units would be made up of experienced personnel who would be trained to investigate crimes retrospectively using the latest technologies. Thus, professional era police agencies typically maintained a distinct separation among those who were assigned to uniform patrol and those who specialized in criminal investigations, and most police agencies continue this bifurcated approach today.

The Rand Institute conducted an evaluation of the criminal investigation process in 1973 in order to determine (1) what types of activities investigators engaged in to retrospectively solve crimes and (2) the degree to which detectives were effective.[63] Among other things, the evaluation discovered that one of the most important factors in determining whether or not an investigation was successful was information that was obtained from the patrol officer(s) who initially responded to the scene.[64] The study effectively debunked the notion that detectives were solely responsible for solving crimes and highlighted the importance of patrol officers in producing successful investigations. Moreover, the findings imply that a larger degree of street-level cooperation among detectives and patrol officers would improve the effectiveness of retrospective investigations.

At the same time, advocates of community-oriented policing reforms became increasingly critical of rotational beat assignments. The act of rotating patrol officers may have arguably led to decreased opportunities for street-level corruption; however, it became apparent that constant rotations in beat assignments also negatively impacted the effectiveness of patrol officers. In particular, officers who were constantly rotated in and out of beats were not afforded the opportunity to get to know the citizens that they policed, nor were they able to gain intimate knowledge of the crime and disorder problems specific to the neighborhood.

As a result, some agencies have moved to what has alternately been referred to as "geographic" or "sector" deployment approaches. For example, agencies that have initiated geographic or sector deployment programs typically begin by dividing the jurisdiction into distinct geographic sectors or zones with one "team" deployed to each zone. While particular plans can and often do vary, each team will typically consist of: (a) a commander, (b) several supervisors who work to manage the team on a day-to-day basis and answer directly to the team commander, (c) several patrol personnel who are permanently assigned to the sector, (d) one or more detectives who are also assigned permanently to work cases in the sector in collaboration with patrol units, and (e) representatives such as traffic and gang unit personnel from other specialized divisions within the department.[65] These personnel then work collaboratively to deal with crime problems within the geographic area.

Other jurisdictions have taken the concept further and have included representatives of numerous community groups as key players in the concept. For example, the approach enacted by the Kansas City Police Department includes leaders of local neighborhood associations, persons who operate businesses in the local area, as well as representatives from neighborhood schools and the city code enforcement office. The program is designed to develop comprehensive community-based partnerships with police to solve problems and address crime issues in geographically distinct areas of the community.[66]

It is common for large agencies to employ this model as well with strong precinct-centered management by captains or upper-level commanders, who have a resource array that is as comprehensive as feasible: Detectives, crime analysis officers, community policing team officers, bike/foot patrol personnel, CRTs, even traffic, mounted or other specialized officers or teams. The precinct, then, becomes semiautonomous, community bounded, and centered, but at the same time the immediate relationship between the chief and upper command staff and the captain/commanders ensures that accountability, strategic direction, and department standards are uniform and consistent. What remains centralized are those specialized functions that, from a practical or operational standpoint, should be shared among precincts: SWAT, bombs, communications, homicide, internal affairs, etc. There is nothing revolutionary in this deployment model; in point of fact, it is becoming the norm for large municipal agencies.

Whichever model is employed, the reality is that crime control requires team work. Crime control in a police agency should never be the function of specialists, no matter how dedicated those specialists may be. Crime control includes coordinated efforts by crime response teams, divisional detectives, investigative specialists, gang units, narcotics units, community policing specialists, and—most importantly—by patrol. Crime control is a team effort centered on patrol. Police resources should be so allocated and so deployed.

ENDNOTES

1. G. J. Sullivan, *Directed Patrol* (Kansas City, MO: Kansas City Police Department); F. Bartch, "Integrating Patrol Assignments: Directed Patrol in Kansas City," in *Review of Patrol Operations Analysis: Selected Readings from ICAP Cities* (Washington, DC: U.S. Department of Justice, 1978); Kansas City Police Department, *Response Time Analysis: Executive Summary* (Washington, DC: U.S. Department of Justice, 1978).

2. W. G. Gay, T. H. Schell, and S. Schack, *Improving Patrol Productivity: Volume*

I-Routine Patrol (Washington, DC: Government Printing Office, 1977); J. S. Yates, "Directed Patrol Systems — The Answer to Critics of Deterrent Patrol." *FBI Law Enforcement Bulletin* 51, no. 12 (1982): 1–9.

3. J. Warren, M. Forst, and M. Estrella, "Directed Patrol: An Experiment That Worked." *Police Chief* 46, no. 6 (1979) 48–49, 78.

4. C. T. Thayer and G. E. Rush, "Crime Reduction: The Tustin Experience." *Police Chief* 50, no. 12 (1983): 47–49.

5. C. D. Brannan, *Denver (CO) Police Department — Special Crime Attack Team (SCAT) — A Demonstration of Directed Patrol Procedures — Final Report* (Washington, DC: National Institute of Justice, 1976).

6. J. B. Howlett, S. H. Killman, and J. B. Hinson, "Managing Patrol Operations: Before, During, and After in Charlotte, North Carolina." *Police Chief* 48, no. 12 (1981): 34–43.

7. Charlotte Police Department, *Managing Patrol Operations: Final Report* (Washington, DC: National Institute of Justice, 1980).

8. Charlotte Police Department, *Managing Patrol Operations*; Howlett et al., "Managing Patrol Operations."

9. J. H. Auten, "Crime Prevention and Police Patrol — Are They Compatible?" *Police Chief* 48, no. 8 (1981): 60–67.

10. W. H. Carbone, *Innovative Patrol Operations* (New Haven, CT: South Central Criminal Justice Supervisory Board, 1975); Warren et al., "Directed Patrol"; W. D. Franks, "Montpelier, Vermont's Directed Patrol Experiment." *Police Chief* 49, no. 1 (1980): 24–26; T. A. Reppetto, "Police Anti-Burglary Strategies in the United States," in *Coping with Burglary*, ed. R. Clark and T. Hope (Boston, MA: Kluwer-Nijhoff Publishing, 1984), 155–67.

11. J. F. Schnelle, R. E. Kirchner, M. P. McNees, and J. M. Lawler, "Social Evaluation Research: The Evaluation of Two Police Patrolling Strategies." *Journal of Applied Behavior Analysis* 8 no. 4 (1975): 353–65; J. F. Schnelle, R. E. Kirchner, J. D. Casey, P. H. Uselton, and M. P. McNees, "Patrol Evaluation Research: A Multiple-Baseline Analysis of Saturation Police Patrolling During Day and Night Hours." *Journal of Applied Behavior Analysis* 10, Spring 1977.

12. New Haven Police Department, *Directed Deterrent Patrol: An Innovative Method of Preventive Patrol* (Washington, DC: National Institute of Justice, 1976); V. G. Strecher, *Goal Oriented Policing: Major Police Studies and Findings* (Huntsville, TX: Sam Houston State University, 1993), Unpublished manuscript.

13. New Haven Police Department, *Directed Deterrent Patrol*.

14. Strecher, *Goal Oriented Policing*.

15. Gay, Schell, and Schack, *Improving Patrol Productivity*.

16. G. W. Cordner, "The Effects of Directed Patrol: A Natural Quasi-Experiment in Pontiac," in *Contemporary Issues in Law Enforcement*, ed. J. J. Fyfe (Beverly Hills, CA: Sage, 1981), 37–58.

17. G. W. Cordner and D. J. Kenney, "Tactical Patrol Evaluation," in *Police Program Evaluation*, ed. L. T. Hoover (Washington, DC: Police Executive Research Forum, 1998), 15–55.

18. L. W. Sherman, D. P. Rogan, and J. W. Shaw, *The Kansas City Gun Experiment* (Washington, DC: National Institute of Justice, 1994).

19. Ibid.

20. L. W. Sherman, P. R. Gartin, and M. E. Buerger, "Hot Spots of Predatory Crime: Routine Activities and the Criminology of Place." *Criminology* 27, no. 1 (1989): 27–55.

21. Ibid.

22. C. Koper, "Just Enough Police Presence: Reducing Crime and Disorderly Behavior by Optimizing Patrol Time in

Crime Hot Spots." *Justice Quarterly* 12, no. 4 (1995): 649–72.

23. Sherman, Gartin, and Buerger, "Hot Spots of Predatory Crime."

24. Koper, "Just Enough Police Presence."

25. Ibid.

26. L. W. Sherman and D. P. Rogan, "Effects of Gun Seizures on Gun Violence: 'Hot Spots' Patrol in Kansas City." *Justice Quarterly* 12, no. 4 (1995): 673–93.

27. D. Weisburd and L. Green, "Policing Drug Hot Spots: The Jersey City Drug Market Analysis Experiment." *Justice Quarterly* 12, no. 4 (1995): 711–35; D. Weisburd, L. Green, F. Gajewski, and C. Belluci, *Policing Drug Hot Spots* (Washington, DC: National Institute of Justice, 1995).

28. L. W. Sherman, D. P. Rogan with T. Edwards, R. Whipple, D. Shreve, D. Witcher, W. Trimble, The Street Narcotics Unit of the Kansas City Police Department, R. Velke, M. Blumberg, A. Beatty, C. A. Bridgeforth, "Deterrent Effects of Police Raids on Crack Houses: A Randomized, Controlled Experiment." *Justice Quarterly* 12, no. 4 (1995): 755–81.

29. Weisburd and Green, "Policing Drug Hot Spots."

30. Sherman et al., "Deterrent Effects of Police Raids on Crack Houses."

31. D. Weisburd, L. Maher, L. W. Sherman, M. Buerger, E. Cohn, and A. Petrosino, "Contrasting Crime General and Crime Specific Theory: The Case of Hot Spots Of Crime." San Francisco, CA: Paper presented at the American Sociological Association Annual Meeting, 1989; L. W. Sherman, "Repeat Calls for Service: Policing the 'Hot Spots,' " in *Police and Policing: Contemporary Issues*, ed. D. J. Kenney (New York, NY: Praeger, 1989), 150–65; J. K. Stewart, *Kansas City Preventive Patrol Experiment: A Hot Spots Replication* (Washington, DC: National Institute of Justice, 1990).

32. G. W. Cordner and D. C. Hale, *What Works in Policing?* (Cincinnati, OH: Anderson, 1992).

33. J. Q. Wilson and B. Boland, "The Effect of the Police on Crime." *Law & Society* 12, no. 3 (1978): 367–90; J. Q. Wilson and B. Boland, *The Effect of Police on Crime* (Washington, DC: National Institute of Justice, 1978).

34. Cordner, *Contemporary Issues in Law Enforcement.*

35. S. E. Martin, "Policing Career Criminals: An Examination of an Innovative Crime Control Program." *The Journal of Criminal Law and Criminology* 77, no. 4 (1986): 1159–182; S. E. Martin and L. W. Sherman, "Catching Career Criminals: Proactive Policing and Selective Apprehension." *Justice Quarterly* 3, no. 2 (1986): 171–92; A. F. Abrahamse, P. A. Ebener, P. W. Greenwood, N. Fitzgerald, and T. E. Kosin, "An Experimental Evaluation of the Phoenix Repeat Offender Program." *Justice Quarterly* 8, no. 2 (1991): 141–69.

36. W. D. McCormick, "Criminal Patrol Techniques." *FBI Law Enforcement Bulletin* 57, no. 1 (1988): 19–22.

37. Ibid.

38. J. E. Boydstun, *San Diego Field Interrogation: Final Report* (Washington, DC: Police Foundation, 1975).

39. Cordner and Kenney, *Police Program Evaluation.*

40. Boydstun, *San Diego Field Interrogation.*

41. Cordner and Kenney, *Police Program Evaluation.*

42. G. P. Whitaker, C. D. Phillips, P. J. Haas, and R. E. Worden, *Developing Policy Relevant Information on Deterrence: Aggressive Policing and Crime* (Washington, DC: National Institute of Justice, 1983); G. P. Whitaker, C. D. Phillips, P. J. Haas, and R. E. Worden, "Aggressive Policing and the Deterrence of Crime." *Law & Policy* 7, no. 3 (1985): 395–416.

43. F. S. Budnick, *Examination of the Impact of Intensive Police Patrol Activities—Final Report* (Washington, DC: National Institute of Justice, 1971); J. S. Dahmann, *Special Crime Attack Team: A Case Study in the Examination of Police Patrol Effectiveness. High Impact Anti-Crime Program* (McClean, VA: Mitre Corporation, 1975); K. Krajick, "Evidence Favors Aggressive Patrol." *Police Magazine* 3, no. 5 (1980) 30; G. P. Whitaker, C. D. Phillips, and A. P. Worden, *Aggressive Patrol: A Search for Side-Effects* (Washington, DC: National Institute of Justice, 1984); R. E. Worden, G. P. Whitaker, and C. D. Phillips, "The Administration of Deterrence: Bureaucratic Structure and Aggressive Policing," New York, NY: Paper presented at the National Conference of the American Society for Public Administration, 1983.

44. W. G. Skogan, *Disorder and Decline: Crime and the Spiral of Decay in American Neighborhoods* (Berkeley, CA: University of California Press, 1992).

45. L. W. Sherman, "Police Crackdowns: Initial and Residual Deterrence," in *Crime and Justice: An Annual Review of Research, Volume 12*, ed. M. Tonry and N. Morris (Chicago, IL: University of Chicago Press, 1990), 1–48.

46. V. E. Henry, *The COMPSTAT Paradigm: Management and Accountability in Policing, Business, and the Public Sector* (Flushing, NY: Looseleaf, 2002); E. B. Silverman, *NYPD Battles Crime: Innovative Strategies in Policing* (Boston, MA: Northeastern University Press, 1999).

47. O. Burden, "Ain't Too Proud to Beg: Of Squeegee Men and 'Broken Windows'." *Law Enforcement News* 20, February 1994, 6; W. Smith, "Don't Stand So Close to Me." *Policy Review* 70, Fall 1994, 48–54.

48. L. T. Hoover and T. J. Caeti, "Crime Specific Policing in Houston." *Texas Law Enforcement Management and Administrative Statistics Program Bulletin* 1, no. 9 (1994): 1–12.

49. J. Houston, "What Works: The Search for Excellence in Gang Intervention Programs." *Journal of Gang Research* 3, 1996, 1–16; C. M. Johnson, B. A. Webster, E. F. Connors, and D. J. Saenz, "Gang Enforcement Problems and Strategies: National Survey Findings." *Journal of Gang Research* 3, 1995, 1–18; M. W. Klein, *The American Street Gang: Its Nature, Prevalence, and Control* (New York, NY: Oxford University Press, 1995).

50. Johnson et al., "Gang Enforcement Problems and Strategies"; M. W. Klein, "Attempting Gang Control by Suppression: The Misuse of Deterrence Principles," in *The Modern Gang Reader*, ed. M. W. Klein, C. L. Maxson, and J. Miller (Los Angeles, CA: Roxbury, 1993), 304–13.

51. I. A. Spergel, *The Youth Gang Problem* (New York, NY: Oxford University Press, 1995).

52. R. P. Owens and D. K. Wells, "One City's Response to Gangs." *Police Chief* 58, 1993, 25–27; J. P. Rush, "The Police Role in Dealing with Gangs," in *Gangs: A Criminal Justice Approach*, ed. J. M. Miller and J. P. Rush (Cincinnati, OH: Anderson, 1996), 85–92.

53. Klein 1995, *The American Street Gang.*

54. Klein 1993, *The Modern Gang Reader,* 312.

55. R. Rush, G. Shelden, S. K. Tracy, and W. B. Brown (1997). *Youth Gangs in American Society.* Belmont, CA: Wadsworth; Spergel, 1995.

56. E. J. Fritsch, T. J. Caeti, and R. W. Taylor, "Gang Suppression Through Saturation Patrol and Aggressive Curfew and Truancy Enforcement: A Quasi-Experimental Test of the Dallas Anti-Gang Initiative." *Crime and Delinquency* 45, no. 1 (1999): 122–39.

57. Ibid.

58. M. Haller, "Historical Roots of Police Behavior." *Law and Society Review* 10, 1976, 303–23.
59. Cordner and Hale, *What Works in Policing?*
60. Boydstun, *San Diego Field Interrogation.*
61. M. J. Hickman and B. A. Reaves, *Local Police Departments, 2003* (Washington, DC: U.S. Department of Justice, 2006).
62. Haller, "Historical Roots of Police Behavior."
63. P. Greenwood and J. Petersilia, *The Criminal Investigation Process:* *Volume 1: Summary and Policy Implications* (Washington, DC: U.S. Department of Justice, 1975).
64. R. H. Langworthy and L. F. Travis III, *Policing in America: A Balance of Forces* (Upper Saddle River, NJ: Prentice Hall, 2003).
65. See e.g., Michigan State Police. (2007). Available at www.dpps.msu.edu; Miramar Police Department. (2007). Available at www.miramarpd.org.
66. Kansas City Neighborhood Alliance. (2007). Available at www.kcna.org

CHAPTER

7

Deployment in a New Era of Policing: The Evolution of Operational Strategies

By the late 1960s, the decades-long movement to reform and professionalize police had reached a crossroads. The movement that began at the turn of the twentieth century with upper-class elites demanding an end to endemic patronage and political corruption had continued unabated through the middle of the century with the likes of O. W. Wilson and other police reformers who successfully centralized police organizational structures, improved the quality of police personnel, and implemented new and more efficient crime control tactics.[1] In the midst of spiraling crime rates and violent rioting that had erupted within many of the nation's large cities, it became clear that the movement to reform and professionalize police had somehow gone awry.

Calls from researchers and community leaders to "halt reform in its tracks" began with the growing recognition that while the movement to reform police had worked to increase the status of the profession and sever ties that had promoted political corruption, the process of reform had *also* resulted in a burgeoning rift between the police and the communities they were supposed to protect and serve.[2] For example, reform and professionalization had resulted in police forces that had become unrepresentative and largely unresponsive to community concerns, and the costs associated with reforms in terms of rising salaries and growing benefits had become anathema to inflation-weary taxpayers and budget-conscious city administrators. Communities—especially those within the nation's urban minority neighborhoods—had become increasingly alienated from the professionalized police.

Over the course of the ensuing three to four decades since community alienation initially became an issue, contemporary law enforcement administration has been engaged in an ongoing, evolutionary process of change toward strategies that seek to increase collaboration between communities and the police. Changes began to emerge during the 1970s with experiments in what was then referred to as "team policing," an attempt to mitigate street-level corruption and bridge the growing rift between officers and the general public. By the early 1980s, police agencies were experimenting with foot patrol as a means to capture some of the attributes of the old-style pre-reform "beat cop" who personally knew members of the public and was intimately tied to the precincts that they patrolled.

Likewise, during this period, researchers and police administrators began to use the term "community-oriented policing" (COP) to describe a wide range of tactics that aimed to control crime and community disorder through collaborative strategies that challenged police to engage citizens. As part of this movement, police administrators began to recognize the importance of expanding the police role beyond reactive crime fighting to include more proactive approaches intended to prevent crime and reduce fear.

By the early 1990s, the widespread acceptance of the COP model seemed beyond dispute given survey results that indicated a strong willingness on the part of police executives to adhere to the COP model's dominant tenets and implement strategies consistent with the philosophy such as the use of storefront ministations and the creation of community policing "specialists" and crime prevention units. Rather than calming the proverbial waters of debate concerning how the police should operate on the street however, the emergence and wide-scale acceptance of the COP model seems to have recently prompted *more* new ideas and additional strategies, including such things as the use of Compstat, in addition to the emergence of modern deployment tactics such as directed patrol, hot spot patrol, and zero-tolerance policing. While some have argued that a number of these newer strategies represent a shift away from the larger COP model, the fact that new ideas continue to appear regarding how police should be managed and the manner in which they should engage citizens lends credence to the notion that policing is currently engaged in what organizational theorists refer to as a "paradigm shift," or a period in which operational experimentation is challenging the established beliefs of the profession.[3]

If what has been occurring over the course of the last 30 years in policing can properly be referred to as a paradigm shift—and we think it can—then we need to consider how the wide variety of new philosophies and strategies have or likely will impact the administration and deployment of patrol units. For example, how has the creation of specialized units dedicated to community policing functions impacted the workload of traditional "beat" officers within a given agency? How will communities react to "zero tolerance" police patrols designed to aggressively maintain public order? Can focused "hot spot" patrols fulfill the promise of crime reduction? These and countless other issues necessarily accompany the current paradigm shift, a movement that has provided police administrators an almost endless array of options to consider in terms of devising a coherent patrol philosophy and possible tactics to be implemented. The goal of this final chapter is to familiarize the reader with many of these newer patrol philosophies and their parallel strategies, as well as suggest ways in which the ongoing paradigm shift and range of tactics that has accompanied it may be altering the street-level behavior of patrol officers. In addition, it provides context to answer the question "why, and on what principles or objectives" should police agencies deploy their patrol resources?

EVOLVING OPERATIONAL STRATEGIES

This chapter will cover changing trends in "operational strategies," a term we use to describe what Cordner[4] referred to as "the key operational concepts that translate philosophy into action." That is, we cover some of the broader strategies that stand in contrast to the old professional model of policing including: (1) problem-oriented policing (POP), (2) the "broken windows" thesis, (3) Compstat, and (4) intelligence-led policing.

Problem-Oriented Policing

Herman Goldstein[5] developed Problem-Oriented Policing (POP) drawing from research conducted in the 1970s, as well as his own personal experiences. He argued that over the long course of the professional era police had become an incident-driven and reactionary force, a situation that seriously hampered the ability of police to prevent criminal activity before it occurred. Essentially, POP shifts the focus of patrol operations away from merely responding to calls for service by urging officers to look for underlying problems that create the calls for service in the first place. POP represents a change from traditional "incident-driven policing," with its reactive posture that places a high value on getting in and getting out of calls for service as quickly as possible. Instead, Goldstein[6] argued that the police must engage the community to begin to police itself. The model he proposed brought together three inter-related interests: (1) tapping the accumulated knowledge and expertise of police officers; (2) enabling officers to realize a higher level of satisfaction in their jobs; and (3) enabling the citizenry to realize a higher return on their investment in the police. The ultimate objective of the POP model is to reduce both the number and the impact of calls for service that emanate from particular problems.[7]

In the POP model, officers are expected to "problem-solve," a process that should include (1) identification of problems by recognizing the relationship between specific crime events, (2) a systematic analysis of information relating to the problem using a wide range of sources, (3) an exhaustive search for solutions to the problem including those found outside the criminal justice system, and (4) an ad-hoc evaluation of each problem-solving approach.

Several research studies have examined the effectiveness of POP; however, none is more well known than the Newport News study conducted by Eck and Spellman.[8] The Newport News Police Department implemented a POP philosophy to deal with three problems: burglaries at an apartment complex, automobile break-ins at a parking lot, and prostitution in a downtown business area. In Newport News, the officers worked closely with residents, business owners, and a variety of other governmental services to deal with the aforementioned problems. In regards to the parking lot burglaries, the officers discovered that the cars were parked by naval personnel while they left on long duty assignments. They also discovered that there was inadequate lighting and supervision at the lot. New lighting was installed in the parking facility and the police increased patrols around the area which significantly reduced the break-ins. Saturation patrol and zero-tolerance tactics were introduced in the downtown areas which essentially removed the problems with prostitution; however, this problem was most likely displaced to another area. Finally, several environmental improvements and other tactics were implemented at the apartments which had some effect. In the end, however, the apartments were razed and the residents relocated to other areas.[9]

Several other pieces of research have examined the POP process and implementation. The evaluations of the Baltimore COPE project,[10] Troy, New York,[11] and San Diego[12] all show impact from the implementation of POP on crime and disorder in these communities. Although the evaluations are positive, rigorous designs and statistical evaluations are lacking in many of the studies assessing POP. In particular, the long-term effects of these programs and changes in philosophy are not yet known.[13] Finally, there are remaining practical concerns for any police administrator who is interested in truly integrating the problem-solving approach agency-wide. Specifically, can beat officers who patrol high-crime beats afford to take the time to problem-solve when they are also expected to rapidly respond to calls for service that often occur one after another?

Resource allocation and deployment decisions have an important impact on any approach a department takes to policing. It is particularly important in a POP environment because you're not only working to create discretionary time but trying to direct the use of that time toward problem-solving activities. Every police administrator has heard patrol officers say they agree with the idea—they just do not have the time to _____ (fill in the blank) whatever it is the administrator wants them to do. Officers will say they are running from call to call and hardly have the opportunity for a meal break—there just isn't time to do problem-solving. In some cases they are right. In others, it is the perception of constant business, and in still others it is just a way to avoid change. The resource allocation and deployment process is a crucial step in structuring a department to implement a problem-oriented philosophy of policing.

The Broken Windows Thesis

In 1982, an article entitled "Broken Windows: The Police and Neighborhood Safety" appeared in the March issue of the popular periodical *The Atlantic Monthly*.[14] The article's appearance coincided with the momentous shift toward COP that occurred within most of the nation's police agencies, and the subsequent impact of the "broken windows" thesis would reverberate for decades to come. Similar to the earlier-introduced POP model, Wilson and Kelling's[15] broken windows thesis generally argued for the need to enact proactive patrol tactics that stood in contrast to the reactive model that had resulted from the professional era reforms. Wilson and Kelling borrowed heavily from the theoretical work of Shaw and McKay,[16] early twentieth-century theorists who developed what has come to be known as the "Chicago School" of criminology, a theoretical tradition that focuses on the crime-producing structural characteristics endemic to socially disorganized urban neighborhoods.

The broken windows thesis proposed a developmental sequence or "spiral of decline" that occurs in economically marginal neighborhoods that make these areas "ripe for criminal invasion."[17] Wilson and Kelling[18] theorized that a parallel existed between what they referred to as "untended property and behavior" (e.g., physically decayed buildings, panhandling, loitering, public intoxication) and the onset of serious predatory crimes such as assault and robbery within a given location. The existence of physical disorder (i.e., broken windows) and these social incivilities work to weaken or decrease informal social control mechanisms within a community, such that neighborhood residents increasingly do not care about the community they live in or the well-being of coresidents. In reaction to this decrease in levels of informal social control, fear of crime among these residents increases. Eventually, the loss of informal social control and parallel rise in fear of crime produces what Wilson and Kelling refer to as "community atomization," or the isolation of coresidents from one another. In effect, residents physically withdraw from their communities and socially withdraw from one another, thereby creating an area that is conducive to the commission of predatory street crime.

For Wilson and Kelling, the primary basis for providing a theoretical groundwork for their thesis was to pave the way for arguments concerning how police—specifically patrol officers—can collaborate with the community to halt the spiral toward serious crime. In contrast to the professional era's reactive model, the broken windows thesis argued that patrol officers can begin to remedy the spiral toward serious crime by using aggressive order maintenance tactics against the relatively minor acts of social incivility described above. Patrol officers should work with community members to define acceptable standards of behavior that conform to community norms. For example, officers should remove undesirable persons such as vagrants and drunks from a neighborhood when they violate community norms and increase perceptions of disorder. As various forms of social incivility are halted, the latent informal social control mechanisms of the community should be reinvigorated and the threat of invasion from serious criminal activity should be lessened. In short, policing in accordance with the broken windows thesis emphasizes the use of aggressive, proactive tactics by patrol officers in an effort to insulate communities from serious crime.

As the COP model gained widespread support among police administrators, the central tenets within the broken windows thesis—that is, that there is a demonstrable link between the physical and social deterioration of communities and the onset of violent crime, as well as the belief that collaboration between police and the community can sever that link—quickly became accepted. Some researchers, however, have been more reluctant to concur and have pointed out some issues in terms of both the broken windows argument and the broader COP model that should be of concern to police administrators interested in altering the behavior of patrol personnel.[19] For example, there is evidence to indicate that typical residents in low-income urban neighborhoods are extremely reluctant to cooperate with police in producing crime reduction strategies. So too, it may be overly optimistic to believe that intermittent police–citizen interaction can mitigate the larger structural and economic ills that plague these types of communities.

Compstat

During the mid-1990s, the New York City Police Department coined the phrase Compstat, which stands for COMPuter STATistics. Since then, Compstat and its progeny have begun to revolutionize how police agencies across the country gather, manage, and disseminate crime data and optimize the crime-fighting capability of street-level patrols. The then New York City police commissioner William Bratton devised Compstat as a "goal-oriented management process that builds upon the police organizational paradigms of the past and blends them with the strategic management fundamentals of the business sector."[20] The Compstat model is driven by the use of a computerized information system that processes, maps, and disseminates crime data throughout the police agency. The primary objective is to increase organizational accountability for addressing crime and disorder problems by facilitating the flow of information from police administrators to command-level personnel.[21] Compstat is intended to empower police through the use of modern information management systems so that they can proactively control crime and disorder. In this respect, Compstat and similar information-driven models can be viewed as part of the larger trend away from the reactive model of policing that was dominant during the professional era.

Bratton and Knobler[22] describe four key principles of the Compstat model: (1) accurate and timely intelligence, (2) rapid deployment of resources, (3) the implementation of effective tactics, and (4) ongoing assessment of effectiveness. The model creates four distinct levels of accountability within the police organization.[23] First, agency administrators and executives exchange information with precinct commanders. These meetings involve an analysis of crime statistics for the precinct, as well as a critical interview and evaluation with the command-level personnel regarding outcomes for the preceding time period and the development of strategies to improve outcomes in both the short and long term. Second, command-level personnel interview and evaluate subunit commanders. Third, subunit commanders interview and evaluate sergeants concerning how they allocate resources and enact street-level strategies to impact crime trends and disorder problems within their jurisdiction. Finally, sergeants are charged with working directly with street-level patrol units to implement the overall strategy.[24]

The system devised and implemented in New York City has received wide-scale acclaim, and many have credited the model as the primary factor in producing a 50 percent drop in New York City's crime statistics for the seven major index crimes from 1993 to 1998.[25] Likewise, other departments including Newark, NJ; Philadelphia, PA; and Minneapolis, MN that have implemented variations of the Compstat model have also experienced sharp declines in crime.[26] However, questions remain in terms of the relative impact of Compstat in producing these successes given the fact that agencies across the nation that did not implement this model or a variation of this model were also experiencing similar declines during that time period.

Moreover, police administrators who may be interested in implementing Compstat-like strategies should be familiar with some of the more specific criticisms of the model.[27] Compstat appears to work to increase organizational accountability in regards to reducing objectively based crime measures (i.e., official crime stats); however, some have viewed the model's focus on objective crime measures as too narrow and in opposition to some of the core tenets of the COP model. For example, Compstat does not incorporate specific indicators concerning fear of crime within the community, an issue that has long been emphasized by advocates of COP as an indicator of overall police effectiveness independent of objectively based crime statistics. Likewise, the model de-emphasizes the importance of enacting problem-solving tactics to reduce noncrime problems within the community, an issue of importance for those who advocate the broken windows thesis.[28]

Regardless of the criticisms, Compstat implementation is rapidly accelerating. Several major East Coast agencies have implemented Compstat. It was also brought to New Orleans and Miami with promises of invigorating those agencies. The city of Los Angeles hired William Bratton in 2003 as chief of police with the sole purpose of bringing the NYPD Compstat model to that embattled organization. Chicago has implemented a Compstat model focused upon reduction of homicide. It is evident that there has been widespread dissemination of the Compstat approach over the past several years.

From a deployment perspective, Compstat will not work without having some discretionary field resources in reserve. Stated differently, Compstat will not work unless there is a crime response team, tactical unit, or patrol reserve that can respond on immediate notice to particular locations experiencing particular problems. Virtually every one of the advocacy books hammers home the point that Compstat is not community policing, and indeed might well be characterized as the antithesis of community policing. Does an agency contemplating implementation of Compstat have to eliminate every one of its community contact, problem-solving, or crime prevention programs? Clearly not. But if one is going to have the resources available for a crime response team, then a police manager might well have to redline the DARE program in order to gain those resources.

Indeed, Compstat is clearly most effective if there are layers of discretionary resources. That is, various crime problems call for the immediate redeployment of various resources. Some require that gang units be immediately focused upon the issue. Some require that an auto theft unit is able to drop whatever else it is doing and give a least some attention to a developing theft pattern. Some require that generalist divisional investigators be able to refocus some of their effort at least for a short period of time. Some require narcotics to be involved. But if everyone is stretched so thin that there is not an extra minute available from any unit in the police department, an agency might as well skip Compstat altogether. A large proportion of the police department might be better informed about crime patterns and trends in the community, but if one cannot do anything about it, so what?

The War on Terror, Post–9/11 Reforms and Intelligence-Led Policing

Our review of the research concerning evolving operational strategies and modern tactics lends significant credence to the idea that increased police presence can lead to measurable reductions in crime. This finding deals a serious blow to the stance that police are incapable of affecting crime and that increasing the level of police presence has no effect on crime. More than anything else, the research shows that police patrol needs to become more of a "goal-driven" enterprise, one that is supported by relevant and timely crime analysis information. It is no longer adequate for police executives to formulate patrol allocation and deployment decisions on the basis of models that were designed decades ago, or in accordance with "what always has been done" in their particular jurisdiction. Moreover, patrol strategies need to incorporate an evaluation component that is designed to determine what has worked and what has not, so that strategies and tactics can be tailored to the problems that police confront in their particular jurisdiction, and fine-tuned over time. To the greatest degree possible, line officers need to be involved in the planning and implementation of the program from the outset to give these street-level personnel a comprehensive understanding of the strategies and tactics to be employed, as well as provide patrol a "buy-in," or personal incentive to insure that these strategies succeed.

Increasingly, this proactive, "goal-driven" enterprise is likely to be influenced by the aftermath of the 9/11 attacks and the ongoing war on terror. Perhaps it is becoming most appropriate to view the evolution in patrol strategies and tactics as culminating into a movement toward what has been referred to as "intelligence-led policing." The beginnings of this movement certainly include the dissemination of Compstat and other similar models, but they also have been pushed in the aftermath of the devastating 9/11 attacks.[29] The 9/11 attacks and the ongoing war on terror have demonstrated that terrorism respects no jurisdictional boundaries, whether these attacks take the form of aircraft hijackings, the use of biological agents or weapons, or more sophisticated attempts to infiltrate critical infrastructures.[30] This realization has forced local police administrators to focus considerable attention on the need to improve law enforcement intelligence operations. The notion that state and local law enforcement agencies must enhance their intelligence capabilities represents a fundamental shift in the strategic dimension of local policing that involves making these agencies "intelligence-led" organizations reminiscent of the military model used for gathering, assessing, and distributing critical information.[31]

Historically, the intelligence operations of local police have been hampered by a lack of formal policies, procedures, and training related to the collection and analysis of essential crime information.[32] The transformation of local police agencies into intelligence-led organizations involves several key objectives: (1) the creation of a task and coordination process, (2) the development of core intelligence products to lead the operation, (3) the establishment of standardized training practices, and (4) the development of protocols to facilitate intelligence capabilities.[33]

This approach is intended to improve the capability of local law enforcement agencies not only in regards to responding to terror threats, but also in traditional anticrime efforts. Those who advocate a transformation toward intelligence-led policing have argued that many of the strategies traditionally associated with the COP can and should be used to further militarize the intelligence capabilities of local departments.[34] For example, the Scanning, Analysis, Response, and Assessment model, or SARA model, most often associated with POP has been identified as a pillar of the COP movement; however, some have increasingly recognized that the model's collection and analysis focus can also be applied within a broader context to not only "solve problems" in the traditional sense but also enhance the overall intelligence capabilities of local police agencies. In effect, those who believe that local police intelligence operations should operate on the military model have attempted to "blend" intelligence-led policing into the broader COP model that has become the dominant paradigm in policing since the 1980s.[35]

There is some evidence to suggest that these initiatives have already started to alter the intelligence operations of local police agencies. A recent national survey found that a majority of responding local and state police agencies have conducted terrorism threat assessments since 9/11, and about one-third of these agencies have collaborated with the FBI's joint terrorism task force to assist in local crime investigations.[36] The movement toward intelligence-led policing has also been pushed by the creation of "fusion centers," which serve as a "clearinghouse" for all potentially relevant homeland security information that can be used to assess local terror threats and aid in the apprehension of more traditional criminal suspects.[37]

Along with these changes, the 9/11 attacks are likely to continue to transform the role of patrol officers. For example, police executives recognize that federal officials are increasingly expecting local police to investigate suspected terrorists and respond to threats by terror groups.[38] This situation will further complicate patrol allocation and deployment decisions, and increase demands on patrol units that are already stretched to the breaking point in some jurisdictions. Clearly, the expanding nature of the threat from terror groups and the corresponding expansion of the role of patrol officers further highlights the need for utilizing modern, information-based patrol allocation and deployment models.

ENDNOTES

1. R. Fogelson, *Big City Police* (Cambridge, MA: Harvard University, 1977); G. L. Kelling and M. H. Moore, "The Evolving Strategy of Police." *Perspectives on Policing* (4) (National Institute of Justice: Washington, DC, 1988).

2. Fogelson, *Big City Police*.

3. J. Barker, *Discovering the Future: The Business of Paradigms*, 2nd ed. videotape (Burnsbille, MN: Charterhouse Learning Corp, 1991); T. Kuhn, *The Structure of Scientific Revolutions*, 2nd ed. (Chicago, IL: University of Chicago Press, 1970); W. F. Walsh, "Compstat: An Analysis of an Emerging Police Managerial Paradigm." *Policing: An International Journal of Police Strategies & Management* 24, no. 3 (2001): 347–62.

4. G. Cordner, "Community Policing: Elements and Effects," in *Community Policing: Contemporary Readings*, ed. G. Alpert and A. Piquero (Prospect Heights, IL: Waveland Press, 1998), 48.

5. H. Goldstein, *Policing a Free Society* (Cambridge, MA: Ballinger, 1977); H. Goldstein, "Improving Policing: A Problem-Oriented Approach." *Crime and Delinquency* 25 (1979): 236–58; H. Goldstein, *Problem-Oriented Policing* (New York, NY: McGraw-Hill, 1990).

6. Goldstein, *Problem-Oriented Policing*.

7. Eck and Spelman, "Who Ya Gonna Call?"; J. E. Eck and W. Spelman, "A Problem-Oriented Approach to Police Service Delivery," in *Police and Policing: Contemporary Issues*, ed.

D. J. Kenney (New York, NY: Praeger, 1989).

8. J. E. Eck and W. Spelman, *Problem-Solving: Problem-Oriented Policing in Newport News* (Washington, DC: Police Executive Research Forum, 1987b).

9. Ibid.; W. Spellman and J. E. Eck, *Newport News Tests Problem-Oriented Policing* (Washington, DC: National Institute of Justice, 1987).

10. G. W. Cordner, *The Baltimore County Citizen Oriented Police Enforcement (COPE) Project: Final Evaluation* (Baltimore, MD: University of Baltimore, 1985); Eck and Spellman, "Who Ya Gonna Call?" Eck and Spellman, *Police and Policing*.

11. D. Guyot, "Problem-Oriented Policing Shines in the Stats." *Public Management* 73 (1991): 12–16.

12. B. Burgreen and N. McPherson, "Implementing POP: The San Diego Experience." *Police Chief* 57, no. 10 (1990): 50–56.

13. D. L. Weisel, "Playing the Home Field: A Problem-Oriented Approach to Drug Control." *American Journal of Police* 9, no. 1 (1990): 75–95.

14. J. Q. Wilson and G. Kelling, "Broken Windows: The Police and Neighborhood Safety." *The Atlantic Monthly*, March 1982, 29–38.

15. Wilson and Kelling, "Broken Windows."

16. C. Shaw and H. D. McKay, *Juvenile Delinquency and Urban Areas* (Chicago, IL: University of Chicago Press, 1942); C. Shaw and H. D. McKay, *Juvenile Delinquency and Urban Areas*, rev. ed. (Chicago, IL: University of Chicago Press, 1969).

17. Wilson and Kelling, "Broken Windows," 32.

18. Wilson and Kelling, "Broken Windows."

19. See e.g., M. Buerger, "A Tale of Two Targets: Limitations of Community Anti-Crime Actions." *Crime & Delinquency* 40, no. 3 (1994): 411–36;

R. M. Grinc, "Angels in Marble: Problems in Stimulating Community Involvement in Community Policing." *Crime & Delinquency* 40, no. 3 (1994): 437–468; S. Mastrofski, "Community Policing as Reform: A Cautionary Tale," in *Community Policing: Rhetoric or Reality*, ed. J. R. Greene and S. Mastrofski (Westport, CT: Praeger, 1988), 47–67.

20. Walsh, "Compstat," 352.

21. Walsh, "Compstat."

22. W. Bratton and P. Knobler, *Turnaround: How America's Top Cop Reversed the Crime Epidemic* (New York: Random House, 1998).

23. Ibid.

24. Ibid; Walsh, "Compstat."

25. E. B. Silverman, *NYPD Battles Crime: Innovative Strategies in Policing* (Boston, MA: Northeastern University Press, 1999).

26. Walsh, "Compstat."

27. M. H. Moore and A. A. Braga, "Measuring and Improving Police Performance: The Lessons of Compstat and Its Progeny." *Policing: An International Journal of Police Strategies & Management* 26, no. 3 (2003): 439–53.

28. Moore and Braga, "Measuring and Improving Police Performance."

29. G. Healy, *Deployed in the USA: The Creeping Militarization of the Home Front*. The Cato Institute Policy Analysis Series (Dec. 17, 2003).

30. R. W. Taylor, T. J. Caeti, D. K. Loper, E. J. Fritsch, and J. Liederbach, *Digital Crime and Digital Terrorism* (Upper Saddle River, NJ: Pearson Prentice Hall, 2006).

31. Bureau of Justice Assistance, *Intelligence-Led Policing: The New Intelligence Architecture* (Washington, DC: US Department of Justice, 2005); K. Riley, G. Treverton, J. Wilson, and L. Davis, *State and Local Intelligence in the War on Terror* (The Rand Corporation, 2005).

32. Bureau of Justice Assistance, *Intelligence-Led Policing.*

33. Ibid.

34. Ibid.; Riley et al., *State and Local Intelligence in the War on Terror.*

35. Bureau of Justice Assistance, *Intelligence-Led Policing.*

36. Riley et al., *State and Local Intelligence in the War on Terror.*

37. Bureau of Justice Assistance, *Intelligence-Led Policing.*

38. S. Walker and C. M. Katz, *The Police in America: An Introduction,* 5th ed. (Boston, MA: McGraw Hill, 2005).

INDEX